EARTH'S VOICES, TRANSCRIPTS FROM NATURE, SOSPITRA

AND OTHER POEMS

WILLIAM SHARP

Published by Left of Brain Books

Copyright © 2021 Left of Brain Books

ISBN 978-1-396-32018-7

First Edition

Table of Contents

DEDICATED

IN

HIGH ESTEEM AND IN PERSONAL REGARD

TO MY FRIEND,

WALTER H. PATER,

FELLOW OF BRASENOSE COLLEGE, OXFORD,

AUTHOR OF 'STUDIES IN THE HISTORY OF THE RENAISSANCE,' ETC.

THE lines entitled 'Sleepy Hollow' and the Sonnets 'Mnemosyne' and 'La Pia' have already appeared in *The Academy,* and three or four of the 'Transcripts from Nature' in *The Athenæum.*

For courteous permission to reprint the copyright verses called 'The Last Aboriginal' and 'Birchington Revisited,' I am indebted in the one instance to the Proprietors of *Cassell's Magazine,* and in the other to the Editor of *Harper's.*

W. S.

'It is enough to lie on the sward in the shadow of green boughs, to listen to the songs of summer, to drink in the sunlight, the air, the flowers, the sky, the beauty of all. . . . . I want to be always in company with these, with earth, and sun, and sea, and stars by night.'

'The hours when the mind is absorbed by beauty are the only hours when we really live, so that the longer we can stay among these things, so much the more is snatched from inevitable time.'

RICHARD JEFFERIES.

'The *tædium vitæ* results from incapacity to see. . . . . To write the poetry of Ennui is to mistake the first function of the poet, whose special work it is to lend a new seeing to our eyes, to enable *us* to see the glory and the wonder of Nature's largess.'

THEODORE WATTS.

EARTH'S VOICES.

I. HYMN OF THE FORESTS.

WE are the harps which the winds play,
A myriad tones in one vast sound
That the earth hearkens night and day—
A ceaseless music swaying round
The whole wide world, each voiceful tree
Echoing the wave-chants of the sea.

For even as inland waves that moan
But break not 'midst the unflowing green
Our trees are: and when tempests groan
And howl our frantic boughs between,
Our tumult is as when the deep
Struggles with winds that o'er it sweep.

'Neath bitter northern skies we stand,
Silent amidst the unmelting snows,
Gaunt warders of the desolate land:
Silent, save when the keen wind blows
The drifting wreaths about our feet,
Then moan we mournful music sweet.

Or in vast ancient woods of beech
Far south we make Spring's dearest home
The haunt of myriad songsters, each
A living flow'r made free to roam
From bough to bough, and thence we send
A forest-music without end.

1

'Neath tropic suns and ceaseless glow
With orient splendours we are filled:
'Midst Austral solitudes we grow,
Where seldom human voice has thrilled:
And ever and where'er we rise
We chant our ancient harmonies.

For aye the sea sings loud and long
In strange and solemn mystery
A wonderful transmitted song—
The echo of all history—
This song o'er all earth's lands we sing
While round the circling seasons swing.

II. THE HYMN OF RIVERS.

Through all the wide lands of the earth
We journey onward to the sea:
Swift from the hills that give us birth
In melting snows we race in mirth
Down through green meadows joyously,
Through wood and dale and desert lands,
Where bridges span our floods with bands
And cities foul our many strands.

THE NILE.

From Afric depths I come
    With ever mightier flow,
    Thro' deserts vast I go,
Past crumbling cities dumb
    And dead, and Sphinxes fair
    That with a stony stare
    Brood on in old despair.

Past Thebes and Memphis I
   Roll on my turbid flood:
   Tired now of ceaseless blood,
Beneath this blazing sky
   I fain would bring long peace,
   From drought a long surcease.

THE TIBER.

Majestically, like some great song
   That moves unto a choral end,
My yellow waters sweep along
   Through Rome, until at last they wend
   Through lonely Latin swamps till loud
   Sea-thunders greet them glad and proud.

THE RHINE.

Thro' pasture-lands and vine-clad heights
   I curve and sweep—
With memories of a thousand fights
   Lying hidden deep,
With echoes of uncounted wars
   Long laid asleep—
Past ruins of ancient castles grim
   Upon each steep.

A thousand meadows I make green
   With all delight
Of flowers, till cornfields clothe the scene
   Where once the might
And dread and tumult of fierce war
   Filled day and night
With blood and death—tho' now I flow
   With waters bright.

I am bless'd and bless: I crave no more
Than that my waves may onward pour
    Forever thus, and be to all
The best inheritance of yore.

THE THAMES.

Through wooded banks and lovely ways
    My silver waters flow:
I linger long in some sweet place
    Where lilies blow:

Past villages and towns I swim
    With ever-widening size,
Until at last I chant my hymn
    Where London lies.

The commerce of the world I bear,
    Till seaward I have pass'd
And, blent with salt waves, onward fare
    Through ocean vast.

THE MISSISSIPPI.

With mighty rush and flow I sway
For ever on my kingly way,
And sing a new song night and day
Wherever my brown waters stray:

I sing a great land that shall be
The glory of Humanity,
I chant of nations all made free
Under the flag of Liberty:

Old beyond count, yet young am I—
I read the stars that flash on high,
And in their secret signs espy
A great and glorious prophecy.

THE AMAZON.

Through tropic forests and old lands
With ruin'd fanes, past sun-scorch'd sands,
My mighty flood rolls vast and strong,
Chanting a dirge-like ocean song!

THE MURRAY.

Through Austral plains my waters flow,
    Through gum-tree forests deep;
And silently I grow and grow
    Until at last I sweep
A thousand miles through plain and wood,
    Then turn my face to where
I hear the thundering tidal flood
    Boom through the air.

THE GULF STREAM.

From out the Gulf of Mexico
Impetuously my waters flow
And through the fierce Atlantic glide,
A wondrous tepid azure tide—
Till all the lands in the North seas,
Where else the Polar winds would freeze
All life, are filled with warmth and stand
Each like a long-drawn emerald band.
And as from north to south I swing
My song is what the sea-waves sing.

Innumerable, our songs are blent
In one great chorus that is sent,
Now sad and strange, now full of mirth,
In circling music round the earth:
We are the children of the sea,
And we too whisper as we flee
The secret of life's mystery.

III. THE SONG OF STREAMS.

With ceaseless murmur of song
　　We slip through meadow and wood,
And we love to linger long
　　Where old dead cities brood
With stealthy sweep or with swirl
　　Thro' highland and lowland we flow;
In flood-time our waters we hurl,
　　In drought we move shrunken and slow.

We sing, like the birds who beside us
　　Are fill'd with the joy of their days,
And we follow the course that doth guide us
　　Throughout the long length of our ways—
And when in some mightier river
　　Or depths of the sea we are tost,
There also we live on forever,
　　For nought that hath lived can be lost.

IV. THE SONG OF WATERFALLS.

Like veils of mist
　　Adown the hills
We bend and twist
　　In a myriad rills,
And sway and quiver in the air with a thousand rainbow-
　　thrills.

O'er crag and fell
　　We bound in glee,
Weaving our spray-spell
　　Mistily
About the sunlit mountain heights that flash like the
　　flashing sea.

6

Past mountain-vales
And hill-tarns deep,
And pine-wood dales
Where the winds sleep,
We bend, we sway, we quiver with laughter loud, we spring, we sweep.

The winds at morn
Us break in spray;
But we laugh to scorn
Their fierce swift play—
What though they break us at day-dawn, *we* triumph throughout the long day!

We fall and shiver,
Through pools we splash;
We flow like a river
And downward flash,
And loud is our tumult of laughter when over hill-ledges we crash

Deep down thro' the heart
Of a silent wood,
Where the roedeer start
And the wild doves brood,
Filling the quiet greenness there with echoes of hill-strains rude.

From the sun's birth
Till the stars creep
From the dark, our mirth
Doth never sleep,
But ever we bend, we sway, we quiver with joy, we spring, we sweep!

V. SONG OF THE DESERTS.

Wide, open, free, unbounded, vast,
We leagueless stretch the wide world o'er:
Above us sweeps the desert blast,
Or booms the lion's reverberate roar
Or the long howl of wolves that race
Like shadows o'er the moonlit space
In tireless, swift, relentless chase.

We are the haunt of all the winds,
O'er us as o'er the sea they sweep
In boundless freedom: each blast finds
A leagueless waste whereo'er to leap
And race uncheck'd,—and day and night
We hear the wild rush of their flight,
A desert-music infinite.

Ten thousand leagues of grassy plain
We stretch, or trackless wastes of sand:
O'er us no mortal king doth reign,
But Bedouin or savage band
And wild-eyed beasts of prey alone
Wander about our tameless zone,
That bondage never yet hath known.

VI. SONG OF THE CORNFIELDS.

For miles along the sunlit lands
    We sway in waves of gold,—
A yellow sea that past the strands
    Has inland rolled.

The sweet dews feed us thro' the night,
    The soft winds blow around;
The dayshine gladdens us with light
    And stores the ground.

We feed a thousand happy birds,
    The field-mice have their share—
Surely to these the reaping swords
    Some grains can spare.

The deep joy of the joyous earth,
    We feel it throb and thrill;
The sweet return of natural mirth,
    Spring's miracle.

All lands rejoice in us, we have
    A glory such as kings
Might envy—but our gold we wave
    For humbler things.

Our golden harvest is for those
    Who strive and toil through life,
Who feel its agonies, its throes,
    Its want, its strife.

O'er all the broad lands 'neath the sun,
    We spring, we ripen, glow;
The seasons change, the swift days run,—
    Again we grow.

VII. SONGS OF THE WINDS.

1. *The North Wind.*

Across the Polar seas,
    From where the frozen snow
Melts with no summer breeze
    But lieth for ever so,

I come, with surging sound
    And frozen rains that sting,
And lash the wintry ground
    With furious wing.

But when 'tis summer weather
    I cool the sun-scorch'd earth,
And chase the clouds together,
    And laugh with joyous mirth.

2. *The East Wind.*

Keen and relentless
    My blasts sweep across
Where the Baltic billows
    And North Seas toss;

Like bolts from the bow
    In a tumult of war,
They rush and they strike
    Wild coasts afar.

And inland hurrying
    They sweep and they swirl,
And the blossoms of spring
    From the orchards whirl.

And I laugh to hear
    The moan of the trees,
And the sound and tumult
    Of stormy seas.

3. *The West Wind.*

I come from out the West,
And I breathe a breath of rest,
    And the sweet birds greet me singing
From every tiny nest.

I am the wind of flow'rs—
I haunt the wild-wood bow'rs—
    And when my song is ringing
Spring knows her sweetest hours.

But when the autumn days
Grow short, I rise and race
    Thro' all the woodlands, flinging
Strewn leaves o'er every place.

When winter comes once more,
With deep tumultuous roar
    I sweep o'er ocean, bringing
Wild tempests to each shore.

4. *The South Wind.*

From burning deserts bare,
From tropic gardens where
Sweet blooms and spices rare
Make fragrant the warm air,

I come, and o'er the deep,
Where storm-winds no more sweep

But soft-aired breezes creep,
Summer I bear asleep.

Sweet Summer! in her dreams
Her face is fair with gleams
Of thought of running streams,
Of flowers, and moonshine beams.

When I have reached the strand
I lay her on the sand
And blow away sleep's band—
Till, waking, through the land

She runs with eyes aglow
With joy where rivers flow,
Where myriad roses blow,
And leaves wave to and fro.

And after many days,
When o'er the brown burnt ways
That thirst 'neath the sun's rays
She cares no more to gaze,

I carry her again
Back to her Southern plain—
And till spring comes again
I moan and rave in pain.

VIII. THE SONG OF FLOWERS.

What is a bird but a living flower?
  A flower but the soul of some dead bird?
And what is a weed but the dying breath
  Of a perjured word?

12

A flower is the soul of a singing-bird,
    Its scent is the breath of an old-time song:
But a weed and a thorn spring forth each day
    For a new-done wrong.

Dead souls of song-birds, thro' the green grass
    Or deep in the midst of the golden grain,
In woodland valley, where hill-streams pass,
    We flourish again.

We flowers are the joy of the whole wide earth,
    Sweet nature's laughter and secret tears—
Whoso hearkens a bird in its spring-time mirth
    The song of a flow'r-soul hears!

IX. THE WILD BEE.

Where in the fields the new-mown hay
Sweet fragrance makes, I wing my way:
I swing within the pliant fold
Of bindweed-bell, or o'er the gold
Of dandelions and kingcups pass:
At times entangled in the grass
I sip the purple orchis sweet,
Or climb the campion's stalk, then fleet
With gauzy wings and happy hum
Close to the seeding limes have come,
Then off to where the hawthorn blows,
And thence where meadow-sweet thick grows!
All through the day I hum and fly,
My honey-search ne'er cease to ply,
And, when the sunlight passes swift,
Upon the evening breeze I drift
To where within my tiny nest
I safely drowse in well-earned rest.

X. THE FIELD MOUSE.

When the moon shines o'er the corn,
And the beetle drones his horn,
    And the flittermice swift fly,
    And the nightjars swooping cry,
    And the young hares run and leap,
    We waken from our sleep.

And we climb with tiny feet
And we munch the green corn sweet,
    With startled eyes for fear
    The white owl should fly near,
    Or long slim weasel spring
    Upon us where we swing.

We do no hurt at all:
Is there not room for all
    Within the happy world?
    All day we lie close curled
    In drowsy sleep, nor rise
    Till through the dusky skies
The moon shines o'er the corn,
And the beetle drones his horn.

XI. THE SONG OF THE LARK.

    High up in azure heaven
        I sing a magic song,
    And thrill the wild notes sweetly
        In rapture loud and long.

    O joy of azure heaven,
        Of white clouds as they pass,

O joy of sweet flow'rs blooming
Down in the cool green grass.

O joy of winds that bear me—
O burst of song made free—
A fount of songtide spraying
In a purple sea!

O rapture of sweet music—
Too sweet, too glad, too dear—
What mystery, what wonder,
I see and hear!

O joy of perfect singing!
O joy of life made free!
O world-joy, springing, ringing,
Joy, joy, alone I see!

XII. THE SONG OF THE THRUSH.

When the beech-trees are green in the woodlands
And the thorns are whitened with may,
And the meadow-sweet blows and the yellow gorse
blooms
I sit on a wind-waved spray,
And I sing through the livelong day
From the golden dawn till the sunset comes and the
shadows of gloaming grey.

And I sing of the joy of the woodlands,
And the fragrance of wild-wood flowers,
And the song of the trees and the hum of the bees
In the honeysuckle bowers,
And the rustle of showers
And the voice of the west-wind calling as through glades
and green branches he scours.

15

When the sunset glows over the woodlands
    More sweet rings my lyrical cry
With the pain of my yearning to be 'mid the burning
    And beautiful colours that lie
    'Midst the gold of the sun-down sky,
Where over the purple and crimson and amber the rose-
    pink cloud-curls fly.

Sweet, sweet swells my voice thro' the woodlands,
    Repetitive, marvellous, rare:
And the song-birds cease singing as my music goes
    ringing
    And eddying echoing there,
    Now wild and now debonnair,
Now fill'd with a tumult of passion that throbs like a pulse
    in the hush'd warm air

XIII. SONG OF THE NIGHTINGALE.

Keen, through supremest music,
    My song is fill'd with pain:
    Hark! 'tis the same sad strain
That with pathetic cadence thrilled
    The Thracian plain,
When after Procne's flight I sang alone,
And thro' my deathless music sent a dying moan.

What moonlit glades, what seas
    Foam-edged have I not known!
    Through ages hath not flown
Mine ancient song with gather'd music sweet—
    By fanes overthrown,
By cities known of old and classic woods,
And, strangely sad, in deep-leaved northern solitudes?

16

Nightly my song swells forth,
When the grey stock-dove broods
And whirling bat eludes
The forest boughs, and rings and pants and thrills
In passionate interludes—
Too sweet, too sad, O sorrow and old-time pain,
The love, the glory I see, that will not come again.

XIV. THE RAIN SONGS.

1. *The Rains of the Equinox.*

From the gather'd clouds we sweep
With lance-like shafts of rain,
And we lash the sounding deep,
And we scour the sodden plain;
And we wheel like armies vast
With a hissing sound of mirth,
When the thundering trumpet-blast
Of Tempest wakes the earth.

Where the grey seas fume and rave
We rush with stinging sleet,
Till the foam on each white wave
In scatter'd spray flies fleet;
And over the lonely hills
We pass in a driven cloud,
And feed the mountain-rills
Till they surge with clamour loud.

Then past the forest trees
Upon the wind we hurl,
And o'er the low lying leas
In gusts we sway and swirl,
Past hamlet, village, and town,

Till o'er great cities we sway,
And break and stream straight down
In a mist of smoky grey.

2. *Summer Rain.*

When we're slowly falling, falling,
  Through the hush of summer eves,
And the nightingales are calling
  Their sweet notes mid the green leaves,

And the lilac boughs are sending
  Their keen fragrance thro' the air,
And the slim laburnums bending
  With their weight of golden hair,

Then we feel the thirsty flowers
  Uplift their blooms again;
For the kiss of the sweet cool showers,
  And the ebb of sun-heat pain.

And we breathe a breath of healing
  Over all things that we pass;
Till with tired wings we go stealing
  To our sleep in the green grass.

3. *The Torrid Rains.*

Above the sun-scorch'd sands we break
  In ceaseless fall for many days,
And a sweet sound of waters make
  Within the dried-up river-ways.

Far amid lonely deserts wide
  We thrill faint springs with life again,

Where the wild things at dusk may glide,
    And quench at last their thirstful pain.

And when at length the clouds arise,
    They bear us far away to where
Pant similar lands beneath fierce skies
    And furnace-breath of fiery air.

XV. THE SNOW WHISPER.

Softly, silently, through the night
We fall in starry flakes of white,
Like wings that make no sound at all
We downward float and drift and fall;
A myriad downy feathers we,
Shrouding the land mysteriously.
We cover all the hill-peaks grey,
And silently pursue our way
Down mountain valleys where no sound
Echoes along the frozen ground;
We make a thick drift where the sheep
Huddle together in their sleep,
And o'er the weary stag's retreat
We pass and shroud the tracks its feet
Have made, and where the shivering hares
Crouch low we clothe their barren lairs;
Then o'er the hill-side pastures pass
And cover up the meadow-grass,
And on the branches of the trees
Pile thickly till they bend and sway
As though borne down by some strong breeze;
And in the empty nests we lay
Some votive feather-plumes like those
Which once bore up the songs that rose
From every woodland bough; then o'er

The cart-wheeled roadways to the door
Of each farm-house and tiny cot,
With stiffly-ordered garden plot—
Till all the land is clothed with light
Soft shining robes of stainless white.

And when the wintry moon gleams pale
In the cold steel-blue dawn o'er dale
And meadow and hill—and far
In a faint shine the morning star
Trembles from sight—and suddenly
A sun-wave, like a wave o' the sea,
Upwells from the east in a great flood
O'er hill and valley and plain and wood—
Behold, the sleeping earth lies there,
No longer frozen, bitter, bare,
But sacred, white, serenely fair.

XVI. SIGH OF THE MISTS.

We haunt the marge of streams,
    And where the bittern booms
    'Mid twilight marish glooms,
And where the curlew screams

Above dim lowlying fields,
    We drift with motions slow:
    Or trailing swift we go
Where the pine-forest yields

Before the tempest's force,
    And hang in vapoury drifts
    Or trail in ghostly rifts
Amongst the boughs all hoarse

With windy tumult wild:
    Like ghosts, wan, dismal, grey,
    We haunt the dreary way
Where barren rocks are piled:

'Mid valleys dark and dim
    We brood in sunless dells:
    We weave our dreamy spells
Round ancient castles grim.

Aye voiceless, with no sound
    At all where'er we be,
    We drift mysteriously
Or brood along the ground.

XVII. THE RED STAG.

For leagues the purple heather lies
Upon the hills; the brackens rise
Yard high, and from the thorny gold
Of gorse-shrubs swift the kestrel flies
Unsated from the rabbits' hold:
And everywhere the fresh wind sings
A joyous song, a fragrance flings,
And sweeps above the fern and makes
The green fronds toss as when it flakes
The calm sea-silence with white foam—
And swoops from height to height, and clings
To barren crags where nought doth roam
Save we, swift-footed stags, in flight—
With gusty cries it hurls its might
Against those serried peaks that bare
Rise up and know no life-joy fair,
Save when the golden eagle's wings
With rushing sound surge through the air.

Ev'n as these mountain winds are we,
Untamed and tameless, wild and free;
For us the glory of the hills,
Their lonely barren majesty—
For us the surging mountain rills
When melted snow their torrents fills,
The windy heights, the sunlit glory
Of mountain bastions scarred and hoary;
And leagueless moors and mighty lakes,
And each lone pine-clad promontory
Round which the sea a fierce dirge makes—
The children of the hills are we,
Untamed and tameless, wild and free.

XVIII. THE HYMN OF THE EAGLE.

Upon a sheer-sloped mountain height
My eyrie is; from thence my sight
Looks down o'er the wide lands below:
I watch the wild winds swoop and blow
In savage violence—but here
They howl in vain; I have no fear
Who am the lord of this high sphere.

At sunrise on this peak I stand,
And watch the glory flood the land;
And then on mighty wings I speed
Far hence for lowland prey to feed
My clamorous young—though when night falls
Still echo loud their fledgling calls
About these gloomy mountain walls.

I watch the moon rise o'er the sea
And inland sail mysteriously,
A globe of silver fire on high;

Then pulse the planets in the sky,
And flash the stars, and meteors stream:
And then I drowse, to wake with dream
Of prey, and thro' the stillness scream.

XIX. THE CRY OF THE TIGER.

Deep in the jungle-grass I lie
Until the burning sun on high
Hath flamed to death—till shadows fall
And far and wide the bulbuls call.

Then swiftly, with slow waving tail,
I follow some fresh-beaten trail,
Or through the rice-stems wanly green
I watch the peasant, gaunt and lean,

Upon the further river-side:
Or nigh some pool I softly glide
And when the wild-deer seek the ground
I spring with one tremendous bound

And drink with thirsty tongue the hot
Sweet blood, while far off round me trot
The coward jackals with fierce eyes
Watching for remnants of my prize.

With savage mate I haunt the woods
And roam these deadly solitudes,
Howl answering howl, until the night
Is filled with terror of our might.

Twin deaths, we stalk through jungles deep,
With swift fierce cries we bend and leap:
In hollow thunders far away
Our savage howls resound till day.

XX. THE CHANT OF THE LION.

Athwart the burning bronze-hued sands I send my deep
    hoarse roar,
As boom the tidal seas that break upon a barren shore:
Then back the dun hyenas bowl, or fleet gazelles far hear
And like a flying cloud drift swift across the waste in fear:
The distant camels hearken in the long straight caravan,
They know the King who feareth not their puny master
    man.
Through cloudless days of blazing heat, through fiery
    afternoons
I crouch and hear the desert winds moan out their mystic
    runes,
But when the burning orb has set, and in the purple sky
The star of evening leaps and flames and palpitates on high,
Then down unto the desert-pool with stealthy steps I creep,
And mid the tall green rushes bend and bide my deathly
    leap:
At times alone come stealthily the fierce hyenas there,
Or red-eyed wolves the water lap and howl thro' the still air,
Or midst the reeds the leopard's yellow hide, black-
    spotted, gleams,
Or o'er some festering carcase flap gaunt vultures with
    hoarse screams:
At times alone the wild boar comes, or writhe upon the
    ground
The mighty coils of cobras which long fasting hath
    unwound—
Then loud and terrible and fierce my roar booms o'er the
    waste,
And like a great gaunt shadow o'er the moonlit tracts I haste,
But far the yellow zebras snort and spurn my stealthy flight
And like meteors flash and vanish through the lonely night.

But oftentimes the shy gazelles or great-horned fleet-foot
    deer
With wary eyes in companies unto the pool draw near,
And when assured they drink their fill and high their
    antlers fling,
Like a sudden bolt from heaven within their midst I spring:
Or if they come not nigh at all, mayhap the great giraffe
Stoops o'er the wave his mighty neck the longed-for boon
    to quaff,
Then with a sudden roar upon his yellow neck I hurl,
And far across the desert sands rider and wild steed whirl,
Until at last he sways and falls with red tongue lolling out,
And then his quivering breast I tear with one long savage
    shout—
And far and wide thereafter booms across the level plain
My hoarse deep roar, like thunderous surge upon the
    distant main.

XXI. THE HYMN OF MOUNTAINS.

The mighty giants of the world are we;
    High o'er the level lands and seas we rise:
Great winds sweep round our brows majestically
    Save when above the highest clouds, 'mid skies
    Of windless calm, we only hear their sighs,
At times a mere faint hum, as to and fro
They surge through mighty pinewoods far below.

For us long silence and eternal peace:
    The holy garment of the pure white snow
Abides upon our heights where all things cease
    To live, and where no Spring-breaths blow
    A sudden bloom of sweet flowers high and low:
Alone o'er each wide slope and hollow vale
The drifting clouds their purple shadows trail.

Far down amongst the hills that cluster round,
    What solemn stillness reigns, tho' there each gale
Howls like a famish'd wild-beast, and doth bound
    From height to height in vain attempt to scale
    These upper peaks, serene and cold and pale,
Above all violence of night or day,
Grandly supreme, inviolate for aye.

We know the secret of the planets, where
    They leap in flame upon their heavenly way;
We watch the constellations fill the air—
    The meteors flash, as though in Titan fray
    Great Powers launched these burning stars to slay
Rebellious foes in some abyss of space:
These, not earth's puny troubles, meet our gaze.

XXII. THE OCEAN CHORUS.

Sea meeting sea, we circle round all lands
    And chant aloud our old eternal song:
With wild fierce music upon northern strands
    We break, or surge white tropic shores along
And thunder hoarsely our tempestuous boom
    Far inland till the hollow blast has rolled
'Midst distant vales with ominous sound of doom,
    The echo of sea-dirges manifold.

THE BLACK SEA.

Round desolate lands I sway,
    Round promontories bleak,
With tumult fierce alway
    My sullen wrath I wreak.

26

THE MEDITERRANEAN.

Like a vast turquoise I
  Flow flowery lands between:
But oft I moan and sigh
  For what hath been.

THE ATLANTIC.

Deep, turbulent, and wide,
  My waters seldom rest,
But surge in tameless pride
  From east to west.

THE INDIAN OCEAN.

I bear a thousand freights—
  Of these I tribute take:
No spoil my hunger sates,
  My long thirst doth not slake.

THE AUSTRAL SEA.

An ancient land I keep
  That lay unknown for long,
Drowsed in a mighty sleep
  By my monotonous song.

THE PACIFIC.

Empress of seas, I roam
  Amidst a thousand isles
Fringed round with snow-white foam—
  But treacherous my smiles!

THE ANTARCTIC.

Wan waves o'er grey wastes wander
  Where drifting icebergs go;
With sullen surge I ponder
  Upon mine ancient woe.

THE ARCTIC SEA.

Around the Polar world
　　My vast green billows sweep—
Or hopelessly are hurled
　　'Gainst icewalls stern and steep.

Sea meeting sea, one ocean ever flows
　　With one tumultuous chorus-song for aye—
The same although it chants the eternal snows
　　That shroud the grim death of each Polar day,
Or lifts a joyous voice, a tumult strong
　　Where o'er blue waves the wind of summer flees:
Ominous, terrible, glorious is our song,
　　The blended chants and dirges of our seas.

XXIII. THE HYMN OF SUMMER.

Of late I wander'd far o'er southern lands;
　　With lips long parch'd and dry I sang no strain;
But wandering inland from hot barren strands
　　O'er sun-scorch'd mountain and o'er burning plain,
　　Upon drear treeless wastes I moved with pain
Of fiery thirst, and sped athwart the sands
　　　　With eager passionate gaze,
But shivered as alone through the fierce bronze-hued haze
　　The treacherous mirage afar did gleam,
　　And nought I heard but the hyena's scream,
The mournful howl of wolves, and o'er and o'er
　　　　The lion's roar.

But now that thence I come at call of Spring,
　　How sweet the breath is of the fresh blue sea!
My thirst and weariness aside I fling,
　　And feel once more serenely glad and free:
　　Old memories of past joys come to me,

Each hour some reminiscence sweet doth bring:
    And now once more I pass
Through green-leaved forests and o'er soft emerald grass,
    By honeysuckle hedges, cowslipp'd plains,
    Down lovely, winding, interlacing lanes;
And ever as I go earth's joy fulfilled
    Is round me thrilled.

Mine eyes are soft with dreams of happy things;
    Within my breath there is a drowsy spell;
The woods grow warm and still, the stock-dove wings
    Through silent glades where late Spring's miracle
    Awoke the joyous life through grove and dell:
No more with keen electric tremors sings
    The nightingale, though sweet
The yellowhammer yet his glad song doth repeat
    Where far and wide upon the sun-hazed heights
    The prickly gorse still flaunts its golden lights,—
Though still upon the moor the stonechat's cry
    Rings loud and high.

Swift winds upraise my golden tresses fair;
    A fragrance of blown roses floats around;
I sing a low song through the hot sweet air,
    A syren song, such as in old days wound
    'Midst perilous rocks with magic dreamy sound
That breathed of love and rest, of white arms bare
    And wildly dreamful eyes
And snowy breasts, of ancient old-world strains, and sighs
    Of dear delights that almost were too sweet,
    Of falling fairy laughters, elfin feet,
And murmur'd whispers low as furtive breeze
    On sundown seas.

In dusky eves, when in a mazy dance
    The grey gnats hum and o'er each twilit field

The nightjar swoops with sudden dissonance,
　　And drowsy sheep-bells ring across the weald,
　　And 'midst the ripening corn from sight concealed
The corncrake cries, I breathe mine old romance
　　　　O'er meadow, wood, and dale,
And sigh a subtle magic through the moonbeams pale,
　　Till lovers, speechless with their new won bliss,
　　Together cling, as though each lingering kiss
Were an embodied joy that might not be
　　　　Recaught when free.

XXIV. THE HYMN OF AUTUMN.

I love the purple moors and northern hills
　　Where the deer leap and whirling curlews cry;
I love the breath of the west wind that thrills
　　The mountain-pines until mellifluously
　　They send a wild strain through the listening sky:
I love to watch the azure shadows creep
Across the windless surface of the deep.

But more my joy is in the fields of grain,
　　In orchards fill'd with fruit,—the ruddy pear,
Peaches that through September suns have lain
　　And breathed the sweetness of the mellow air,
　　Vines heavy with the purple weight they bear,
October woodlands where the brown nuts fall
And where the redbreasts still their sweet cries call.

But most I love th' autumnal peace that broods
　　When ere the equinox come windless days:
When spreads a golden glory o'er the woods,
　　An amber-tinted crimson-deepening blaze:
　　Ah! then I love to dream of Summer's ways,
And have no fear of Winter stern and dumb,
Because I know sweet Spring again will come.

XXV. THE HYMN OF WINTER.

Southward I come from where eternal snows
  Lie mass'd in frozen continents; before
My wandering feet a bitter wild wind blows,
  And howls o'er ocean-waste and barren shore
  And lonely uplands, till o'er fertile plains
    In fierce tempestuous fury it doth cast
      Its sounding might, and round the homesteads flies
  With fierce auxiliaries of stinging rains
    And icy sleet whirled forth on new-born blast,
      Engender'd 'midst the dark dense vaporous skies.

Far south my herald tempest speeds, and then
  With snow-bewildering steps I softly come
And breathe my deadly breath o'er hill and glen,
  And leave the leafless forest bare and dumb,
  And turn to a moveless wave each amber stream,
    And freeze the lakes and pools to blocks of white,
      And dust with silver frost the meadow-grass—
Wan, deathly, soundless, like a ghost I gleam;
  Intangible, yet nought resists my might,
    But stiffens when with chill blank eyes I pass.

Nature sleeps fast while I relax no breath:
  Within the bleak grey air the very rooks
Wing with infrequent flight: I breathe cold death
  Where frozen kingfishers haunt sedgy brooks
  And where amidst the snow-clad fields the hares
    Shiver, and skylarks with numbed pinions lie
      Songless for ever now on alien ground:
All that was once so joyous wanly wears
  A shroud of white, and mournful melancholy
    In silence broods and hearkens to no sound.

When on some day, after long-falling snow,
    My wild wind wanders from the south again,
I break my frozen spell, and to and fro
    Wander an uncrown'd king, till I am fain
To reach once more my changeless Polar waste—
    And as I northward go with sullen pace
        I hear faint joyous echoes far off ring,
I hear behind fleet dancing footsteps haste,
    And looking back I see the shining face
        And flower-filled hands of bird-surrounded Spring.

XXVI. THE HYMN OF SPRING.

Across the green fields singing
    I lead my joyous way,
A myriad bird-songs ringing
    Above my flower-strewn way:
The white clouds drift above me
    Within an azure sky,
Life stirs and thrills around me—
    I laugh and onward fly!
Adown the lanes and hedges
    The blackthorns turn to snow,
Along brown forest-edges
    The first primroses blow;
A lark rings high and gladly,
    A blackbird whistles sweet,
A speckled thrush sings madly
    Within some green retreat:
With joy the whole land quivers,
    Woods, meadows, hills, and vales,
Swift streams and rolling rivers,
    When nigh my sweet voice hails.
A breath of balm, of healing,
    I follow Winter's strife—

Like death he comes slow stealing,
    But I with songs of life:
I am the transformation
    Of all that long since fled,
The glorious resurrection
    Of Earth's innumerous dead.

NOTE.

The legend of Sospitra had long haunted my imagination: and when, one day in the late spring of last year, lying in a grassy hollow far out on the Roman Campagna, I came across a detailed reference to this legend in one of Ouida's eloquent books, the unexpected occurrence impressed me with such persistency that finally the story expanded into verse.

The legend runs that Sospitra was visited by two spirits in the guise of Chaldeans, and that they endowed her with more than mortal power and knowledge, giving her supremacy over all creatures, and insight not only into the hearts of men, but also into the great laws of the universe. The 'Chaldeans' gave her lordship over herself, so that she could know neither grief nor mortal weakness, lordship over herself and over all things—save Love and Death. Proud, content, supremely wise, she dwelt far from the haunts of her kind, amongst ancient ruins in a lonely desert.

As it is at this point the poem commences, and as the legend is fully evolved before the close, the 'argument' need not here be further extended.

SOSPITRA.

I.

SOSPITRA dwelt amidst the waste,
    Her home a ruined temple was;
Thereby the fiery wild-ass raced,
    There the swift leaping wolf did pause,
But never came there any one
Of all the tribes under the sun.

II.

At dawn she heard the winds arise,
    And knew where their swift wings would sweep
Thro' that long day: athwart the skies
    She watched th' infrequent cloudlets creep,
And saw where in remote lone lands
The rains would break their vapour-bands.

III.

She watched the long growth of the noon,
    The waning of the ample day;
She watched the circling of the moon
    Through splendour of the Milky Way;
Morn, noon, and night, she saw where each
Successive passed, what far-off beach

IV.

Of isle within Pacific seas
    Gleamed silver in the sunrise light,
At the same time when Afric trees
    Stood parched amid the fierce noon's might,
And dusk of evening slowly stole
Where the grey windy north seas roll.

V.

All things before her were laid bare,
    All knowledge and all power she had;
She knew no sorrow, felt no care,
    Had perfect vision, and was glad:
Even as in a glass she saw
The evolution of one law.

VI.

She watched the life of nations grow,
    She heard the sound of puny wars,
Each mockery of triumph blow
    Beneath the same unchanging stars:
She heard the sound of prayers rise,
Felt the old stillness 'midst the skies.

VII.

Within her brain each thought that passed
    Within the minds of men was held;
Her gaze on each new dream was cast,
    To her the mists were all dispelled;
She saw in flawless nakedness
Each truth that man would curse or bless.

VIII.

Far in an old deserted land
    Sospitra dwelt, 'mid columns vast
That ruin'd stood amidst the sand,
    And had stood since that far off past
When Baal fell, and far and wide
The nations mocked his shattered pride.

IX.

There sovereign and supreme she dwelt;
    To her the desert wild things came—
The antelope before her knelt,
    The fierce hyena there grew tame,

The lion wandered there by night
And let her hand caress his might.

X.

The nightingales that sang anear
    Flew to her call; lithe serpents twined
Before her path; and knew no fear
    The grey-green lizards she would find
On broken marble pedestals,
Or clinging to the ruin'd walls.

XI.

She had strange dreams, she felt the throb
    Of the great world-heart pulse and swing;
She heard the low continuous sob
    Which universal death did wring,
Amidst the loud and jubilant strife
For ever echoing from life.

XII.

Her days were calm and sweet and still;
    Her soul, knowing all things, was at peace:
O'er her no breath of mortal ill
    Might blow, nor Time for her increase
The burden of his years: alone,
Death some far day might claim his own.

XIII.

Death, and that other power—Love:
    But death would never come to her,
From earth around or world above,
    If she ne'er turned idolater
Before the face of him whose eyes
Give man his dreams of paradise.

XIV.

And ever when she thought of this
    Sospitra smiled: she saw too clear

The mockery of his transient bliss
    To dread though Love should draw anear:
She saw his myriad worshippers
Tread o'er his countless sepulchres.

XV.

To her all passions were as things
    Of little heed, like leaves that fall,
And which the wind takes up and flings
    Aside: o'er her they had no thrall—
She knew their heights and depths, but wise,
She looked through each with cold calm eyes.

XVI.

But most she loved the mystery
    Of night, when o'er the desert plain
The twilight shadows stealthily
    Grew into darkness, and like rain
The soft dews cooled the ground and made
A new life thrill through each grass-blade.

XVII.

Oft then she wandered from her home,
    And sought the lonely silent sands;
Beneath the stars she loved to roam
    And call to her the wandering bands
Of fleet gazelles, or by her side,
Feel the fierce tawny lion glide.

XVIII.

Or midst the ruins she would sit
    And watch the solemn moonrise fill
The ancient halls, where the bats flit
    Hither and thither, whistling shrill:
And dream that once again Baal's priests
Held here their sacrificial feasts.

XIX.

These when she wished alone for peace:
　　But when the life-blood overbold
Thrilled in her veins and would not cease
　　To stir strange thoughts she scarce controll'd,
She sat within her home—and then
She looked into the souls of men:

XX.

The inmost secret of each soul
　　To her was bare; the hearts of all
She read as she might read a scroll:
　　She saw Death sweep above them all
And ever and again stoop low
And out some flickering life-flame blow.

XXI.

Ev'n as a scroll that was outroll'd,
　　So unto her the wide world lay:
She saw men perish 'midst the cold
　　Of northern lands, and far away
The fierce sun beat o'er deserts wide
And men athirst who gasped and died.

XXII.

She watched the furious tempest sweep;
　　The shattered vessel plunge and bound
Till swallowed up within the deep;
　　She saw the dead men swaying round
And round in the green depths, with slow
Long swing and eyes that nothing know.

XXIII.

She saw the miner in the womb
　　Of the dark earth: the diver slim
Deep down in the strange world of gloom
　　Above the cluster'd pearl-shells swim:

And ever as she heard and saw,
Her soul was fill'd with some strange awe.

XXIV.

How little seemed each living thing,
    How puny life of man—brute—flower:
And yet, how wonderful the Spring
    That with regenerative power
Swept round the earth—how vast, how great,
Humanity confederate!

XXV.

Sospitra saw, and was content:
    What mattered each small life was vain
When all in one great whole were blent,
    When all were links in one vast chain
That rose from earth's remotest sod
And passed the stars and reached to God!

XXVI.

These things Sospitra felt and knew,
    Before her all of life being glass'd:
But when the mortal spirit grew
    Weak with intense keen sight at last—
How gladly then she turned to where
The fresh wind fill'd the desert air,

XXVII.

Felt its keen breath upon her face,
    And how it swept the whitening grass
Like foam at sea, and swooped in chase
    Of the swift deer it could not pass:
How gladly then she sought the flow'rs
Upon the plains, and spent long hours

XXVIII.

In tireless wandering to and fro,
    Ev'n as a white cloud in the sky

Speeds where'er windy currents go:
  She watched the great-wing'd eagles fly,
The wild-ass snort in desert pride
Then stamp and race up to her side.

XXIX.

She wished for nothing more; her heart
  Desired no things she knew of old—
It felt no longing, knew no smart—
  And yet not passionless or cold
Her nature—rather, like a hill
With calm snows clad, whose heart fires fill.

XXX.

But one day a strange restlessness
  Fell on her, and a keen desire
To know the ill or happiness
  Of life herself—to feel the fire
Ev'n though it should consume: but weak
A moment only, with blanch'd cheek

XXXI.

She changed her thought—for well she knew
  That if Love strove with her and won—
Even as a leaf a wild wind blew,
  So would she be: for ever done
The serene glory of her days,
The sight and knowledge of God's ways.

XXXII.

And so the seasons fled: the rains
  Swept from the skies: the winter passed:
And one day o'er the shining plains
  Spring, singing, wandered back at last:
Sospitra, glad, supreme, soul-strong,
Sang back a sweet rejoicing song.

XXXIII.

Beautiful beyond women she:
 Yet never had she felt again
The wish amongst her race to be:
 Safe from all grief, or fear, or pain,
She watched the unswerving laws of life
Move on forever through the strife.

XXXIV.

She looked, and felt her soul expand
 To see Humanity so great—
In power, in will, in faith, so grand—
 Heedless of love or scorn or hate
From Powers it dimly knew—but she
Saw God's Will working ceaselessly.

XXXV.

One eve o'ercast the sky became;
 Great purple-shadowed clouds rose high:
There was a flash, a lurid flame—
 And all the vast vault of the sky
Seemed one great mass of whirling fire,
With crash on crash and tumult dire,

XXXVI.

While a dull hollow roaring sound
 Swept through the heavens—as at sea
A cyclone like a beast doth bound
 Upon the waves, and furiously,
Finding its strength is vainly thrown,
Howls with a long reverberate moan—

XXXVII.

An hour of sound and fire and strange
 Convulsion and bewild'ring riot!
But suddenly there came a change—
 The lightnings ceased, the sky grew quiet,

The shattered clouds were swept away
And faint stars fill'd the twilight grey.

XXXVIII.

Sospitra felt the peace, and slept;
    She dreamed strange dreams: she saw a host
Of spirits, and each spirit wept;
    She saw a bleak and lonely coast
Where one soul evermore did pace—
She looked, and knew her own pale face:

XXXIX.

But last she dreamed that once again
    The Spirits who had come before,
Who gave her power o'er things to reign,
    To be than mightiest king far more—
That these two Spirits came and stood,
With eyes that on her soul did brood:

XL.

And that one spake to her and said,
    'Still is it well with thee? Hast thou
No wish for mortal joys, fair maid—
    Would'st fain fulfil thy days as now?
But, if thou would'st not change, be strong—
For Love and Death have waited long.'

XLI.

Then down through sleep's phantasmal ways
    In dreams she wandered sad, alone,
Until she came to a drear place
    And saw a monumental stone
Whereon she read, *Here lies the dust
Of one who placed in Love her trust.*

XLII.

Then deeper still she slept, and dreamed
    No further dreams the whole night long:

And when at dawn the sunlight streamed
  And woke her, she cried out, 'Yea, strong
I am, and fear nor Love nor Death,
The chill cold touch, nor fiery breath!'

XLIII.

She rose, and with swift footsteps passed
  Between the columns, all aglow
With roseate-hues, and faced the vast
  Reach of the plains, felt the winds blow
About her the sweet desert scent—
Was proud, and glad, serene, content.

XLIV.

That eve upon the waste she spied
  What never she saw there before—
A horseman swaying side to side,
  With reins fall'n down as if from sore
Fatigue—or out of sheer despair
In being on trackless deserts bare.

XLV.

With steadfast eyes awhile she gazed
  And watched the horseman nearer come:
She saw his eyes were dim and dazed,
  His dry parch'd lips were fixed and dumb,
And that upon his clothes there lay
Thick clots of blood from some fierce fray.

XLVI.

Then with a slow strange smile she rose
  And 'midst the temple-columns stood—
A marble goddess in her pose,
  And even as marble was her mood:
And thus she watched the horseman ride
With weary languor to her side.

XLVII.

And he, who had no hope at all
    Save that in this deserted fane
Death would not long abide his call
    Nor hesitate to end his pain,
Stood wearily before the face
He judged the goddess of the place.

XLVIII.

Then suddenly he forth did reach
    His hands, and half in mockery
And half unknowing what his speech
    Might be, he cried out bitterly—
'Oh thou, pale goddess, whose old fame
Is blown away like dust—whose name

XLIX.

'Is rumoured in no lands, and here
    Is less than any flower that springs
To life with each returning year,
    Who art less than these bright dying things
That in the sunlight live an hour—
Less than the least of these thy pow'r:

L.

'Yet ev'n to thee I pray, who now
    Know all prayer to be vain indeed—
To thee at last I bend my brow,
    Who of all other gods take heed
But little—and since He they call
The Lord Omnipotent o'er all

LI.

'Has heard no weary cry of mine
    Upon these desert plains—lo I
Before thee bend, and offer wine
    Of blood, and life's faint ebbing cry

To thee who as a true god must
Rejoice I turn again to dust.

LII.

'The wine of blood and life's last sob
    I lay before thy shrine, who art
So lonely now, I would not rob
    The long despair of thy chill heart
Of such slight pitiful worship as
My soul can give ere it doth pass.

LIII.

'Take thou my life, poor goddess, take—
    Unless indeed some power remain
Of thine old faculty to make
    The pulse of life beat swift again—
Take thou or heal, who standest there
Cold, passionless, serenely fair!'

LIV.

Scarce had he spoken, ere with moan
    Of fear and awe his heart grew still:
He saw a tremor in the stone
    And watched the mantling life-blood fill
The face, and heard a low voice say,
'Whence comest thou who here dost pray?'

LV.

Then with the surge of hope he fell
    Upon his knees, and cried, 'O save
Me now, who by some miracle
    Dost speak, like one who from the grave
Comes back with message to restore
Sweet hope to one who hoped no more!'

LVI.

But with his cry his strength ebb'd fast,
    Prostrate he fell before her feet;

Sospitra thought the life had passed,
    The weary throbbing heart to beat—
But ere long breathed he a slow breath,
And not as one that perisheth.

LVII.

And then as in a dream he rose
    And stagger'd where Sospitra led
His feeble frame to sweet repose,
    Cool water for the wounds that bled,
And food and wine, and slumbers deep
With one to guard and safe watch keep.

LVIII.

But even as they entered where
    Her secret room was, an old wound
Reopened, and he gasped for air
    And gave a cry and once more swooned:
She caught him in her arms, afraid
That Death his final thrust had made—

LIX.

But where his faintly beating heart
    Lay close to hers she felt it throb:—
A moment, and his eyes apart
    Wide opened, and a low glad sob
Broke from his lips, and ere she knew
His arms with sudden strange strength drew

LX.

Her body close to his until
    They stood together breast to breast,
And then she felt his life-blood thrill
    Her own, and knew his hot lips pressed
To hers, and, all her heart aflame,
Heard his mouth utter some sweet name.

LXI.

Then from her arms he fell, and slid
    Upon the couch: some moments she
With strange glad eyes her flushed face hid
    Within her hot hands tremulously,
And then she swiftly bent o'er him,
But as she looked her soul-sight dim

LXII.

And dimmer grew, until no more
    She saw life like a scroll outrolled,
Nor read the strange mysterious lore
    Her spirit brooded on of old:
Her dreams seemed far away to her,
Buried in some strange sepulchre.

LXIII.

She laved his wounds, and brought him wine
    And food, that when he should awake
He might have these things for a sign
    He lived indeed, and might partake
And gain his past strength back, and be
Once more his old self verily.

LXIV.

And then Sospitra left, and through
    The silence of the dusk she went;
She saw the same stars in the blue
    Dark vault, she felt the same sweet scent
Blown from the wide free plains, saw race
The swift deer fleeing from place to place—

LXV.

The same, and yet to her how strange
    They were: they did not seem her own
Familiar sphere, or else some change
    Had over them a dim veil thrown,

As evening mists rise up and steal
And make the landscape seem unreal.

LXVI.

No thoughts were hers, but many sighs:
    One prayerful voice alone she heard
'Midst all the universe; her eyes
    Saw one who gazed, whose sudden word
Had lit a fire within her veins
And thrilled her with ecstatic pains.

LXVII.

Long while she wandered to and fro
    In this dream-mood, then slowly turned
And sought the room where he lay low
    Whom she had saved: a soft flame burned
Therein, and by its crimson light
She saw he slumbered still, death-white.

LXVIII.

And as she watched, sleep came on her;
    She in a dreamless slumber lay
As if entranced; no sounds there were
    In that still place, though far away
The hoarse hyenas on the plain
Howled in their savage hunger-pain.

LXIX.

And while she slept, he woke: strange awe
    Filled him at first—he dimly thought
This was a goddess whom he saw
Beside him, whose pure face he sought
    With questioning eyes and heart that thrilled,
But ever with a fear that chilled.

LXX.

But as the strange magnetic gaze
    Of human sight can ev'n control

The mind of one whom fevers daze
    And waken the sense-clouded soul,
So in her sleep Sospitra stirred,
And muttered dreamily one word—

LXXI.

The one word *Love*, and through her eyes
    Two single tears came forth, and low
From parted lips breath'd sudden sighs:
    But he who watched, with heart aglow
With sudden exultation cried,
'No goddess she who here beside

LXXII.

'Me dreams, no prophetess austere!
    No goddess ever yet did keep
A mind a mortal swayed, no tear
    A goddess ev'n in secret sleep
E'er knew, no sad sighs ever moaned
Nor even in dreams Love's lordship owned!'

LXXIII.

And with his low exulting cry
    Sospitra woke, his last words still
Like dream-sounds echoing mockingly—
    Love's lordship—how the words did fill
Her heart with a delirious bliss
And all her old calm strength dismiss!

LXXIV.

Then as a rain-cloud comes on swift
    Aërial wings across the vault
Of heav'n, and the grey rain-mists drift
    Till the lost wayfarer, at fault,
Succumbs and drops—so fever drew
A mist across his mind and blew

LXXV.

Phantasmal visions o'er his sight,
    Until his struggling soul sank far
In darkness, as when clouds at night
    Hide the keen pulse of fieriest star:
For days he lay thus, till at last
One eve the fever ceased and passed.

LXXVI.

The ebb of strength returned and flowed
    Till the new life felt sweet and strange:
While day by day Sospitra glowed
    With lovelier beauty: some swift change
Had turned the seer into a woman,
Made the divine calm heart grow human.

LXXVII.

One eve they sat together where
    Beyond the fane two palm-trees stood:
There was a stillness in the air,
    Not ev'n the desert-wind did brood
Afar; and neither spoke nor stirred,
Each vaguely waiting some swift word.

LXXVIII.

Slowly above the level waste
    The full moon rose and sailed on high:
At times swift sudden meteors raced
    And flashed athwart the solemn sky:
The planets pulsed in fire, and bright
The starry hosts shone through the night.

LXXIX.

Long silent they, till overhead
    A burning meteor swung through space,
A crimson flame that flashed and sped:
    Then swiftly turned they face to face,

And with one low sweet cry she knew
His lips were press'd to hers and drew

LXXX.

Her soul to his: she felt his breath
    Come quick and hard—and glad, elate,
Her spirit cried—'If this be death,
    Lo, than poor Life how much more great!'
Then passionate ardours swept her soul,
As a wind sweeps o'er waves that roll:

LXXXI.

She clung to him, she felt each kiss
    Like flame her very being fill,
She quiver'd with the strange new bliss,
    She felt it throb, and pulse, and thrill—
She knew the Passion of Love, and fell
A slave'neath its resistless spell.

LXXXII.

O hours thereafter and strange night—
    How sweeter far than the old dream,
To yield beneath Love's conquering might!
    Could any after-glory stream
Upon the soul that would not be
Compared with this a mockery!—

LXXXIII.

So thought Sospitra: and for days
    In this long ecstasy of love
She dwelt, content alone to gaze
    Upon her lover's face above,
To hear the music of his words, to feel
Sweet rapturous longings o'er her steal.

LXXXIV.

The days and weeks went past; till he
    Felt weary for his life of old:

The time grew long monotony,
　　Passion wax'd faint and then lay cold
And dead: and one day far he rode
But never sought the ruin'd abode

LXXXV.

Again, nor her who erewhile gave
　　Him life, and thereby also laid
Her greatness in a deep sure grave.
　　Ev'n as a flower doth droop and fade
Sospitra paler grew, faint, weak—
She could not cry aloud nor speak

LXXXVI.

A single prayer: she had no pow'r
　　At all as she of old-time had:
To her brought now the midnight hour
　　No wondrous visions: she grew glad
No more with fervour of high thought,
God's mystic ways no more she sought.

LXXXVII.

A woman now, she knew that Death
　　Would follow Love, and for his rest
She sighed with many a bitter breath:
　　Till one night words came—'It is best:
I would not love's sweet dream undo,
h ough thus his mockery I rue.

LXXXVIII.

'I also am of those who live
　　A brief swift span, who pass away
With all life's passions fugitive;
　　But ah, in that miraculous day
When all Life's complex mysteries
Were clear unto my steadfast eyes,

LXXXIX.

'I saw, as I might read a scroll,
   That death was but a change, a birth,
A rest, and that th' enfranchised soul
   Reached to a higher life on earth—
That ever upward, upward, went
The soul in its divine ascent:

XC.

'Therefore I fear no more at all;
   Therefore I do not cry again
For the old glory I let fall
   From out my life: through joy, through pain
I shall reach onward, till once more
My life is as my dream of yore.'

XCI.

Slowly the long dull hours went by:
   No more Sospitra far and wide
Roved o'er the plains, but listlessly
   She watched the days to evenings glide,
The moon succeed the sun, the stars the moon,
Each slow dawn lead to fiery noon.

XCII.

Death came to her one lonely eve
   And looked upon her pale sad face:
'Though Love doth pass, I shall not leave
   Thee ever in my silent place,'
He whispered gently through her sleep,—
Then breathed o'er her his slumber deep.

XCIII.

The wind blows there with hollow sound;
   The circling seasons bring no change:
When sweet Spring's breath along the ground
   Wakens the flow'rs, no footsteps range

The fragrant ways, no song is heard
Save the shrill music of some bird.

XCIV.

The ruined columns, stone by stone,
   Stand silent 'midst the desert vast:
There the hyena howls alone,
   Or swells the fierce sirocco-blast
Or the dull roar of lions, like sea
Calling to sea monotonously.

NOTE.

These 'Transcripts' (including the selection in the latter part of this volume), like those which appeared in *The Human Inheritance: And Other Poems*, are portions of a series forming a kind of private *Liber Studiorum*, and are here inserted in no natural sequence, but almost at random. This, while practically a necessity on the part of the selector, is calculated to afford more diversity of interest to the reader.

As a rule, but not invariably, I have used the detached couplet which finishes each 'Transcript' as the means of some supplementary touch, heightening the effect by bearing in some way or other upon the broad outline produced in the preceding six lines. The 'Transcripts' are uniform throughout, save slight modifications of the final couplet in Nos. x. and xiv.

FIRST SERIES.

TRANSCRIPTS FROM NATURE. (*First Series.*)

I. TROUTLING.

IN the clear grey-brown stream the reeds
    Rise like tall branchless pines, and glades
    Are there, where in the twilight shades
Like flowers seem the water-weeds:
And to and fro amidst the slim
Reflected leaves the troutling swim

Like birds amongst the trees, but sing
No song, and flit on noiseless wing.

II. THE WASP.

Where the ripe pears droop heavily
    The yellow wasp hums loud and long
    His hot and drowsy Autumn song:
A yellow flame he seems to be,
When darting suddenly from high
He lights where fallen peaches lie:

Yellow and black, this tiny thing's
A tiger-soul on elfin wings.

III. IN A GARDEN. (*Midsummer.*)

Above the beds of mignonette,
    Or 'midst the wall-flowers' drowsy spells
    Or swaying in Canterbury bells
The brown bee hums: o'er wild-thyme wet

With streamlet sprays, the dragon-fly
Hangs blue-black 'gainst the azure sky:

And like blown wild-rose leaves alow
White butterflies drift to and fro.

IV. THE KINGFISHER.[1]

'Neath drooping grasses slips the stream,
   And on a bulrush bending low
    The 'bird of March' sways to and fro
A-shimmer in his sunlit gleam;
Some splendid orchid seems he there,
Soft swaying in the bright Spring air,

With yellow iris-flowers around
And gold marsh-mallows o'er the ground.

V. FIREFLIES. (*In the Ardennes.*)[2]

Softly sailing emerald lights
   Above the cornfields come and go,
    Listlessly wandering to and fro:
The magic of these July nights
Has surely even pierced down deep
Where the earth's jewels unharmed sleep,

And filled with fire the emeralds there
And raised them thus to the outer air.

VI. THE FIREFLY.

The short sweet Tuscan twilight dreams
   Into the reverie of night—
    Darkness and stillness, save a light
That comes and goes with sudden gleams;—

A living flame, an unborn soul
Slow wandering towards an unspied goal,

Thus in its shining devious flight
The firefly seems to me to-night.

VII. TANGLED SUNRAYS.

Aslant from yonder sunlit hill
    The lance-like sunrays stream across
    The meadows where the king-cups toss
I' the wind, and where the beech-leaves thrill
With flooding light they twist and turn
And seem to interlace and burn,

Until at last in tangles spun
'Mid the damp grass their race is run.

VIII. A RAIN-MIST ON LAKE LUGANO.

Dark as the night,—and still as though
    The mountain-shadows lying there
    Defied the wind's power to lay bare
Their haunts of endless sleep,—below
The rugged hills Lugano lies,
No longer blue beneath blue skies:

But o'er it broods a filmy mist,
Stone-grey just touch'd with amethyst.

IX. MOUNT PILATUS. (*Thunder, without wind or rain.*)

A livid blue-black pall, with streaks
    Of lurid light, doth darkly frown
    Above Pilatus looking down
With sovran scorn on lesser peaks;

Wan shifting lights upon these lie—
But no rains fall, no wind-wings fly

Though now the steel-blue lightnings flash
Where the scarr'd peak withstands the crash.

X. MUSIC AND MOONLIGHT. (*Lake of Lucerne.*)

The violet wavelets ripple in
    Upon the shelving shore; and through
    The scented limes a glimpse of blue,
The purple-blue of night, I win:
Yonder Lucerne lies mass'd, all white
In the full moon's redundant light,

And happy laughter comes on fleet
Aerial wings, and echoing music sweet.

XI. SIGNA.

Thro' winter and thro' summer's days
    Hoar Signa dreams her old-time dream:
    The olives make a silvery gleam
About her sun-white hillside ways
And the old houses mellow-toned.
Widowed, still sitteth she enthroned,

Still watches Arno's swift stream flee
With dead leaves to the Pisan sea.

XII. A BOULDER. (*On the Roman Campagna.*)

A sea of billowy green around—
    Above, the hollow azure dome:
    This rock, half buried in the loam,
Has reached, man knows not how, this ground:

Time-worn, and scored as with sea-shells,
It doth not heed the blue harebells—

The twin blue butterflies at rest—
The lizard—on its old grey breast.

XIII. SUNSET ON THE MAREMMA.

Vast tracts of swamp and desert-land
    Stretch leagueless onward from the hills:
    No broad stream flows, but sluggish rills
Crawl thro' the moss and marsh and sand:
No sign of life, save one black crow
That on a tireless wing doth go

The whole one crimson hue, from gleams
Blood-red, the dead sun's dying beams.

XIV. A SIROCCO NOON: FROM SAN NICOLETTO.

As through a silver-woven veil
    Of gauze, I see Venezia gleam
    Thro' the June heat; a soft blue gleam
Shifts o'er the shallow sea; a sail,
Of saffron with a strange device,
Hangs idly where a shallop lies

Moveless:—o'erhead the acacia-blossoms turn
I' the faint wind; around, the poppies burn.

XV. THE LAGUNA MORTA.

Above, the intense blue of the sky—
    Flawless, save that a white gull wings
    Seaward—soundless, save that there rings
A rapturous lark-song from on high:

But all around a dead drear waste
Stretches for miles—rank swamps ungraced

By life, save where the yellow newts
Revel 'midst ooze-fed marish roots.

XVI. A VENETIAN SUNSET: BEFORE A CHANGE.

(*Returning from Torcello.*)

In violet hues each dome and spire
    Stands outlined against flawless rose
    O'er this a carmine ocean flows
Streak'd with pure gold and amber fire,
And through the sea of sundown-mist
Float isles of melted amethyst:

Storm-portents, saffron streamers rise,
Fan-like, from Venice to the skies.

XVII. AN 'IMPRESSION.'

(*Midnight, on the Laguna di Mestre, under the long railway bridge spanning
the distance between Venice and the mainland.*)

A hundred arches left and right
    Are mirror'd in the calm lagoon;
    The stars pulse there, and the gold moon
Sails through a nether sphere of night:
A distant roar—a flame—a crash—
A whirling fiery bolt—a flash—

The train is gone; the echo's o'er;
The arch'd lagoon is still once more.

XVIII. THE SOUTH FORELAND. (*Stormy Sunset.*)

Across th' ensanguined sea the sun
   Sinks slowly through the blood-red west;
   The wind hath moaned itself to rest;
A star leaps forth—the day is done;
Far down below the tide doth lift
Itself against the cliff, with swift

Resurge adown the shingly shore
And hollow, deep, resilient roar.

XIX. SEA-SHALLOWS.

The slow tide rises up the rocks
   Waving the seaweed to and fro,
   The amber tresses in their flow
Seeming like those long mermaid-locks
In which drown'd sailors lie adream:
Between them little fishes gleam,

And clouds of wavering shrimps o'er bars
Of sand, and fork'd slow-moving stars.

XX. THE NINTH WAVE.

Lying here upon this rock whose base
   The grey sea keeps, I watch the waves,
   Wind-driven and rebellious slaves,
Sweep hither in their reckless race:
Now one dies, now another rears
And breaks in countless briny tears,

But one, the ninth, green, hollow, vast,
Towers ere it falls, defying the blast.

XXI. THE CAVES OF STAFFA.

(Gale from the South-West.)

The green Atlantic seas wash past
  The mighty pillars of basalt
  A vast sea-echo through the vault
Swells like a captive thunder-blast;
The wind fierce show'rs of spray doth sweep
Through the cave's gulf, and loud the deep

Resistless billows in their course
Thunder within in tumult hoarse.

XXII. LOCH CORUISK. *(Skye.)*

The bleak and barren mountains keep
  A never-ending gloom around
  The lonely loch; the winds resound,
The rains beat down, the tempests sweep,
The days are calm and dark and still,—
No other changes Cor'uisk fill.

Scarce living sound is heard, save high
The eagle's scream or wild swan's cry.

XXIII. THE AFTERGLOW. *(Canary Islands.)*

The purple twilight dwelleth long
  Amid these western isles, and fills
  The ocean with a peace that stills
The soul, as with their strange sea-song
The old-time syrens soothed away
The unrest of an earlier day:

The crescent moon and one large star
Hang o'er the Afric coast afar.

XXIV. SUNSET AT THE AZORES. (*Against the Orange Groves.*)

Across the Atlantic's moving gold
    The aerial floods of sunset flow,
    Till all the orange-orchards glow
As if earth's ingots hither rolled
Were mass'd, the giant task being done,
To get a last touch from the sun:

The sky-gold reddens—redder shine
The groves, as steeped in ruby wine.

XXV. ON THE THAMES EMBANKMENT.

(*Cleopatra's* Needle.)

Through centuries where the fiery sun
    Of Egypt scorched the desert sands,
    Greeted alone by Bedouin bands,
The obelisk beheld Time spun
Through generations as though hurled
Down the long slope of a dead world:

Now here it stands; but doth it see
For England Egypt's destiny?

XXVI. EMPIRE. (*Persepolis.*)

The yellow waste of yellow sands,
    The bronze haze of a scorching sky!
    Lo, what are these that broken lie,
Were these once temples made with hands?
Once towers and palaces that knew
No hint of that which one day threw

Their greatness to the winds—made this
The memory of Persepolis?

NOTE TO '*GASPARA STAMPA.*'

Gaspara Stampa—the Venetian Sappho as she has been called—was one of the most poetic and fascinating personages of the poetic and fascinating times in which she lived. The friend of Titian and Sansovino and others of that brilliant company who made Venice for a time the centre of the highest civilization, she had also every personal qualification—genius, beauty, culture—save that of patrician birth. Loving, and for a time loved by the Count of Collalto, one of the princeliest and most accomplished of the nobles of Venice, she was unfortunate in having her passionate love ill-rewarded. The Lord of Collalto, while on a mission to Paris, was there enthralled by the famous Diane de Poitiers, and this becoming known to Gaspara so preyed upon her life that, after writing many beautiful, dignified, and pathetic verses and sonnets, in which she embalmed her disastrous passion, she died, or, as is sometimes said, poisoned herself, in the full bloom of her lovely and accomplished youth.

For my first acquaintance with the incidents of her life and the subjects of her verses (which I was fortunate in making before going to Venice) I am indebted to the eloquent little essay by Mr. Eugene Benson, the well-known American painter, residing in Rome. This essay prefaces a number of admirable translations of Gaspara Stampa's sonnets, by 'George Fleming,' the author of 'A Nile Novel,' etc., the whole forming a little book which was published in 1882, by Roberts Bros., of New York.

In the following lines I have merely endeavoured to give four representative scenes from the life of Gaspara, founded partly on her own statements and partly on strong probability. (*See also Notes.*)

If so slight a thing were worth dedicating, the writer would have asked his friend, Mr. Eugene Benson, to let him associate it with his name—not only as a mark of personal regard, or as an acknowledgment of indebtedness, but also from the high opinion he has of Mr. Benson as an artist.

GASPARA STAMPA.

Saffo de' nostri tempi alta Gaspara.

I. *At San Salvatore.*[3]

ADOWN its stony sunwhite bed
The hill-stream slipp'd—not as it sped
In winter when it raged along
In reckless ecstasy of song,
Nor as in early Spring full fed
By melting snows—but shrunken thin
And with a dreamy murmuring sound
Betwixt the rocks and stones it wound:
It sang the cool joys of Cadore,
It whisper'd lowly o'er and o'er
The secrets which the flowers had lain—
The flow'rs of the Trevisian plain—
Upon its wavelets knowing they
Would reach the great sea one sure day,
That sea of which they vaguely knew
As where their song-bird lovers flew
When the sweet months had gone and all
The land was no more musical.

The blue Venetian Alps rose sheer
And stretch'd far north, divinely clear,
Height blending into height until
It seemed as if the wave would fill
And break and sweep in azure flood
O'er mountain, meadow, and vale, and wood.

Above the wild Piavè's stream
An ancient cedar dreamed its dream
In windless silence solemnly,
Rememb'ring how the swift years fly,
How brief the life of flower and bird
And man, how futile every word
Of love, whether of wooing wind
Or mated songsters when they find
Their nests wind-swept, or men who vow
Time shall be unto them as now.
And midway in its vast deep shade,
Cool, fragrant, dark as greenest glade
In some old forest, hand in hand
Two lovers sat, with eyes that scanned
Each other as with eager thirst
The traveller in some lone land
Beholds a visioned paradise
Nor knows the vision then accurst.
There was a wonder in her eyes,
A wonder that such joy could be
For her, and all the world not see
The glory that upon it dwelt:
Holding her lover's hand she felt
The wide green earth a transient dream,
And Time an evanescent gleam,
And Fate an empty sound that blew
About the windy wastes of space,
And Death a shadow faint that flew
Far off with an averted face.

Ev'n as a flower she was, so fair,
So sweet and delicate and rare:
A face that one might see in dreams,
With deep dark eyes whose sudden gleams
Flashed straight from the pure soul within;
And like a halo was the hair

In golden glory gather'd where
The lily-neck rose white and thin.
A lily seemed she verily
To him whom all men thought to be
The perfect rose of manlihood:
Within the eyes that oft did brood
Upon Gaspara's loveliness
Life ever burned in passionate mood;
The very joy of joyousness,
The lust of life was his, the glow,
The fervour which in youth some know
When all life's joyous fragrant flow'rs
Hedge the glad way whereon we go,
Heedless of Time's relentless hours.

So sat the twain one autumn day
In the cool cedarn shade whence they
Looked down where the Piavè flowed
Beneath, and past the sun-scorched road
That led to white Collalto, high
Against the azure of the sky,
Amongst its olive-groves, upon
The blue heights reaching on and on
Till lost in that aerial haze
Which is the breath of autumn days:
Behind them the Trevisian plain
Lay bathed in light, its fields of grain
Like sheets of shimmering gold, and far,
With the swift sparkle of a star,
Where a broad band stretch'd wide away
The azure Adriatic lay.

Long had they silent sat; for love
Broods on itself, ev'n as a dove
Dreams scarcely crooning o'er its peace:
Love scorns poor words, it hath release

In silence. When at last he broke
The silence with the words he spoke
It seem'd to both as if the hour
Were filled with some magnetic pow'r,
Some vivid, keen, electric force
That drew them each to each,—as though
Twin leaves they were in one strong flow
United 'midst a torrent's course.
'Love, love,' he cried, and bending low
He kiss'd the tremulous lips again
And yet again till the sweet pain
Of yearning in her eloquent eyes
And the soft magic of her sighs
Set his hot heart aflame to hold
Her lovely body in embrace,
To feel her arms his frame enfold,
With breast to breast and face to face.

Sweet hours, too soon they passed away.
The glory on the plain grew grey
And Twilight stole with misty feet
From purpling hill to hill to meet
The swarthy darkness as it came
With one bright starry signal flame:
Then hand in hand the lovers went
Up the steep hill-side path to where
The castle's moonlit towers leant
Against the purple-shadowed air.

II. *At Titian's House in Venice.*[4]

As the sun set o'er the low land
Where Mestre lies, a goodly band
With Titian held festivity:
Slowly a glory changed the sea
Till o'er each broad lagoon there rolled

A tide of purple, crimson, gold,
Or delicate amber: far away
The blue aerial hills rose clear
Beyond where the north islands lay
Bathed in soft purplish light; more near
Burano and Murano gleamed,
And where by San Michele drear
The buried dead of Venice dreamed
A sudden saffron splendour streamed.

All were the guests of Titian there:
Gaspara Stampa, noble, fair;
Irene, beautiful and young,
For whom the fierce Tedeschi swung
Their swords; and Palma's famous maid,
Violante of the golden hair;
Cornelia who so often played
Sweet tunes to still the strange unrest
Her brother knew: and for the rest,
Varchi was there, and Bembo whom
With Sansovino 'midst that room
Titian most loved, the tall fair slim
Molino, and anigh to him
The lord Collalto debonair,
And lastly with a mocking air
Pietro Aretino, who
Made most men his keen rancour rue.[5]

Swift gondolas upon the tide
Like swans went past, and far and wide
The tinkling of the vesper bells
Rang clear, or came in low soft swells
Across the calm lagoons; at times
A voice rose singing idle rhymes,
Or a clear lute or mandolin
Played one of those old tunes that win

Our souls to memories of past years
And fill the eyes with sudden tears.

A brief while all sat hushed and still,
Till Aretino rose to fill
His neighbour's glass: then Titian spake—
'When from such silence we awake
Is it not even as we had seen
Some strange new thing, as we had been
Within the heavenly places where
Pure spirits fill the holy air?'
'Yea,' Sansovino said, 'we see
Then: at other times we dream.
But Aretino laughed, 'To me
Such moments pleasant are, they seem
Restful indeed, but more of earth
Than heaven, a breathing-space for mirth
To rest herself, for thought to sleep,
A time the delicate wine to keep
Within the mouth until we catch
Its subtlest flavour, even to snatch
Some moments' slumber. Come, we're fain
For music—let's do life no wrong:
Fair Violante, sing that strain
Of mine I made for singing long
Ago and called "The Syren-Song."'

(*Violante sings:*)

There where the lotos scents the drowsy day,
And hushful fountains fall in ceaseless spray
And strange bright birds their sweet songs sing alway—

I dream, dream, dream of something sweet and dear,
But when I dream I dream in secret fear.

72

The great gold-hearted lilies lie alow
Upon the gliding waters as they flow,
Like white moons in a liquid sky they glow.

Upon a bank of violets I lie
Watching the purple shadows flitting by,
And dream my dream's fulfilment is anigh:

And the cool waters kiss my white limbs fair,
And all about me falls my veil of hair,
And some strange longing fills me unaware.

But here at night, anigh the whisp'ring stream,
I lie amid the lotos-lilies' gleam,
And feel the sweetness of some coming dream.

As when a nightingale doth sing
At twilight and repeated sweetness fling
Far thro' the dusky woods, so sang
The singer with a voice that rang
Far out across the twilit sea,
Now clear and strong, now hushfully
With magic in the low sweet notes:
The fisher-folk within the boats
That southward sailed swift crossed and prayed
As though indeed some Syren maid
Sang a too sweet prophetic tune.

Then slowly rose th' autumnal moon,
Golden and round, and made a track
Of ever-changing silver where
The tidal wash of the lagoon
Swept past the islands, purple-black
Already in the dusky air.
And smilingly Collalto took
His mandolin, with one swift look

To where Gaspara sat with eyes
That answered with a glad surmise:

(*Collalto sings:*)

> *While sways the restless sea*
> *Beyond the shore,*
> *And the waves sing listlessly*
> *Their secret lore,*
> *And the soft fragrant air*
> *From off the deep*
> *Scarce stirs thine outspread hair,—*
> *Sleep!*

> *Far up in purple skies*
> *Great lamps hang out,*
> *White flames that fall and rise*
> *In motley rout;*
> *While fall their silvern rays*
> *O'er crag and steep,*
> *Woodlands and meadow-ways,—*
> *Sleep!*

> *While the moon's amber gleams*
> *Gild rock and flow'r,*
> *Let no untimely dreams*
> *Possess the hour:*
> *Let no vague fears the heart*
> *'Mid slumber keep,*
> *In dreams love hath no smart,—*
> *Sleep!*

When he had ceased, with a slow smile
Scarce hiding its malicious guile
Pietro Aretino said,
'To whom, fair lord, to which sweet maid

Were these words sung? For surely she
Will answer with swift courtesy?'
But even as he spake and sneered,
Gaspara turned with eyes that feared
No mocking, but with far-off gaze
Sang, with a strange light on her face:[6]

> *I gaze into thine eyes*
> > *And gazing there behold*
> > *The glory of Paradise:*
> *Only one fear can make my hope grow cold,*
> *Only one dread within my heart still lies—*
> *Would'st thou wert mine to my last hour to hold!*

> *O fair and fatal face,*
> > *That steals my soul away,*
> > *O sweet divinest grace:*
> *O miracle of love—that thou should'st pray*
> *My heart's desire, that knows no little space*
> *Wherein it never doth thy rule obey.*

But with a sudden evil look,
Lent Aretino o'er, and took
From off its place a small guitar,
And said, 'Love is a fallen star:
We do not well to rant and rave
Of what is soon quenched in the grave,
Which doth not break death's silence, nor
Arise, when once the tomb's closed o'er.
I call it what it is: a thing
To have awhile, laugh, jest at, fling
To the winds again—but never I
Pray for Love's lordship endlessly.
Here is my song:—'
> But Titian said,
'Nay, is not Love that seed God laid

75

Beyond the gates of Paradise—
An Eden-flower to grow and rise,
Which whoso gathereth shall know
His soul is no mere empty breath,
Nor closed stand the Gates of Death?'

Then Bembo: 'Love is God's first seal
To sanctify the soul's advance:
Death is the next.'
                              'And when we feel,'
Gaspara said, 'Love's quenchless fire,
We fall not but we reach up higher:'

'Love is a Spirit of Desire,'
Collalto cried, 'it kills or saves:
Lords are we of it or else slaves.'

To whom, Molino: ''Tis a dream
Wherein we catch a transient gleam
Of some life past or yet to come:
It is the flower of things, the sum
And head'—whereat laughed loud again
Swart Aretino, 'Be it pain,
Or peace, or joy—here is my strain:—'

> *Love is a burning flame:*
> *It feeds on shame:*
> *Lust is its other name,—*
> *Love is a bitter flame.*
>
> *Love dwells in no one heart:*
> *It hath a poison'd dart,*
> *And leaves a bitter smart*
> *In the bruised heart.*
>
> *Love is a bitter thing,*
> *An empty jest to fling,*

A lewd song to sing,
Love is a bitter thing—

A bitter thing, a flame,
It feeds on shame:
Lust is its other name—
Love is a burning flame.

III. *At Murano.*

From garden-ways that to the sea
Sloped down'neath many a cypress tree
A sound of laughter came,—for there,
Rejoicing in the sweet spring air,
A joyous company was met:
But two by a white parapet
Together stood, Gaspara one,
The other, he who late had won
A happy meed of generous praise
For the sweet beauty of his lays
To subtle thought and music grown;
Together there they stood alone,

Tall slim Molino in the flower
Of his full fame, she in the power
Of her acknowledged loveliness.
The cool wind touched with light caress
The soft gold of her lovely hair,
And lovelier than the flower most rare
Transplanted from the east that grew
Within these gardens was her face.
A certain sadness left its trace
Within the dreamful eyes, for he,
He whom she loved so steadfastly,
Far hence 'made glad the land of France:'⁷
To him life was a wide romance,

77

To her 'twas one sole episode:
He had fair paths—she one straight road.

She knew not why her friend thus chose
To turn awhile aside from those
Who loved and honoured both: but glad
She was to ask if aught of news
Of the good lord Collalto had
Of late been heard—with some excuse
Of careless interest as though
His very name sent not a glow
Throughout her face: but with no smile
Molino turned his face awhile
And spake not—all his heart being thrill'd
With sorrow and his dark eyes filled
With tears that he who loved her so
Should be her messenger of woe.
Well knew Molino whom she loved,
Well knew he that she looked unmoved
On him, although with kindly eyes
And sweet familiar courtesies
She met him ever—well he knew
The lord Collalto her heart drew
Unto his life, as the moon draws
The waves of ocean without pause—
And bitterly he cursed this lord
That idly tossed aside his word
And for an untrue woman's sake
Forsook one true, one fit to make
A man's life fair and strong and sweet.

None joined them there with wandering feet,
But long a strange vague silence lay
Betwixt them, as 'tween windy day
And night a silence oft doth dwell.
At last Gaspara cried—'O tell

Me quick this thing you have to say:
He is not dead whom I so well
Have loved and love!'
                                    'He lives, but he,
O dear, sweet friend, hath turn'd from thee:
Be strong! I would to God that vain
My words were, that this dreadful pain
Might then not seize thy tender heart.
Gaspara—friend—no words my tongue
Would e'er have utter'd to thy hurt,
Had I not feared some coarse jest flung
Or that some heedless fool might blurt
The truth out unawares: dear friend,
Forgive me when I say an end
Hath come upon thy high pure love—
For he hath thrown it as a glove
Aside—he is not worthy thee,
Who long hath loved him faithfully!'

'Molino, I adjure thee by the trust
I have in thee, all kindness thrust
From out thy speech and let me have
The bitter truth that nought can save!'

'A famous courtezan has made
His weak heart captive: he has laid
Honour aside, and knows no more
The love he vowed thee o'er and o'er.
In rumour you have heard her name—
Diane de Poitiers—heed her shame
And his no more, Gaspara! Dead
He is to thee whose heart has bled
In bitter ruth to hear.'
                                    'Alas!
I know it to be true: Love has
For women ever a fierce thorn

Behind each flow'r; a bitter scorn
In Hope disguised: O true good friend
I pray thee take me hence. The end
Is come. The dream is dreamed. It is
An old, old song. O life's poor bliss!'

(*Aretino crosses the path, singing:*)

> *Love dwells in no one heart:*
> *It hath a poisoned dart,*
> *And leaves a bitter smart*
> *In the bruised heart.*

> *Love is a bitter thing,*
> *An empty jest to fling,*
> *A lewd song to sing,*
> *Love is a bitter thing.*

IV. *The Last Journey.*

Nigh where the barren sandy shore
Of Malamocco met the roar
And surge of the tempestuous sea,
Gaspara lay. Her misery
Oft led her thither, where no eyes
Would watch her grief, and where her sighs
Unnoticed fell. For miles the strand
Stretch'd bleak and bare—a waste of sand
Where only the sea-poppies grew,
And where the wailing sea-birds flew
Like ghosts of the unburied dead
Lying fathoms deep: for leagues outspread
The foam-swept Adriatic lay,
Until it met the sky-line grey
And sky and sea grew one dull waste
Wherethro' the riotous tempest raced.

All day she lay there like a flower
Rent from its place by the wind's power
And broken: nor as time waned fast
And the fierce tempest wheeled and passed,
Saw she the peaceful afternoon
Bring transient rest ere once again
The changing wind and driving rain
Swept the sea-spray o'er each lagoon.
At last even of this second pain
Of silence she grew tired, and so
She rose and wandered to and fro
Where the cold grey insistent waves
Swung heavily upon the shore:
And murmuring to herself she said,
'O happy they that in their graves
Lie still and quiet, who feel no more
Life's bitterness: O happy dead!
Would God I in my narrow bed
Slept the long sleep, and heard no sound
At all, and no remembrance found,
No tears, no sighs, no ghostly past,
No kiss that turns to dust at last,
No bitter mockery of love,
Nor foiled Hope leaving all aghast
The shivering soul: to hear above
No sound, not even the sweet birds,
For it might chance some stinging words,
Some lover's vow, might reach me there
And I should know the dreadful air
Of life once more, and feel again
Slain Love's intolerable pain.'

And then she knew that she would see
No morrow: and the mystery
Of coming death brought such release
From grief, and such a sense of peace,

It seemed to her as if even then
She died, as if the world of men
Were a past dream, and she were free:
So then she made this song,[8] that he
Might one day read and know how well
She loved—

> *'To suffer grief is to be strong,*
> *And to be strong is beautiful and rare:'*
> *'Twas in thy court, O Love, I learned it there,*
> *This sad, sweet song!*

> *No one man dwells thy ways among,*
> *Who shall not learn thy thousand ways of grief*
> *Or how wild fears succeed each poor relief*
> *In dark'ning throng:*

> *There too a man may learn to put away*
> *The crowned summit of his heart's desire—*
> *But O, the bitter burning of love's fire—*
> *Its bitterer ashes grey!*

Swift in the waning afternoon
Her gondoliers o'er the lagoon
Urged the frail bark until they passed
The Way of the Slaves and glided fast
Before the wave-washed stairs that led
Where 'Santa Maria' rose on high
In domed majestic symmetry.
Westward, beyond the broad canal,
The blue-black sky was like a pall
Drawn straight and smooth, with one broad span
Of ominous orange-gold that ran
Mid-way: and, nearer, fiery drifts
Of crimson cloud with fringe-like rifts,
Ev'n as serrated seaweed swings

In the strong flow of a swift tide,
Swayed to and fro, while overhead
Dull bronze and lurid purple spread
And intermingled. One white flash
Fill'd the whole sky with fire, and crash
Followed tempestuous crash, and blaze
Streamed after blaze, till fire and sound
And Venice all were interwound.
And as the gondola flew fast
Up narrow ways it darted past
Swart Aretino's palace where
He sat at meat with friends and quaffed
His wine, and mocked, and loudly laughed
To see the dread upon each face:
Then hummed unto himself a space,
And sang:—

> *Love is an ended song;*
> *A cruel wrong;*
> *Love lasts not long:*
> *'Tis an old-time song.*
>
> *Love is a bitter thing,*
> *An empty jest to fling,*
> *A lewd song to sing:*
> *Love is a bitter thing.*

MATER DOLOROSA.

SHE, brooding ever, dwells amidst the hills;
Her kingdom is call'd Solitude; her name—
More terrible than desolating flame—
Is Silence; and her soul is Pain.
Day after day some weightier sorrow fills
Her heart, and each new hour she knows
The birth of further woes.
And whoso, journeying, goes
Unto the land wherein she dwells for aye
Shall not come thence until have passed away
For evermore the bright joy of his years.
She giveth rest, but giveth it with tears,
Tears that more bitter be
Than drops of the Dead Sea:
But never gives she peace to any soul,
For how could she that rarest gift bestow
Who well doth know
That though in dreams she can attain the goal,
In dreams alone her steps can thither go:—
Solitude, Silence, Pain, for all who live
Within the twilit realms that are her own,
And even Rest to those who seek her throne,
But these her gifts alone:
Peace hath she not and therefore cannot give.

SONNETS FOR TWO PICTURES BY ROSSETTI.

I. MNEMOSYNE.

SHE looks, in vision, upon some dead thing
With steadfast eyes, subtly interpretive
Of somewhat wonderful that once did live
Beneath soft alien skies in some old Spring—
She hears the laughter that shall no more ring,
    She hears the words no lips shall ever give
    Again in twilight moments fugitive,
She knows the pain that long since lost its sting.

Her right hand holds the lamp of memory
    Low burning, and behind her dies the day
        As dies for her the present. Hush! she hears
Some antique time-forgotten mystery,
        Known only where the swart priests used to pray
        In shrines that were grown old in ancient years.

II. LA PIA.*

'Ricorditi di me che son la Pia;
    Siena me fe' disfecemi Maremma;
        Scalsi colui che inanellata pria
    Disposando m'avea colla sua gemma.'

                         DANTE.

She sits behind the rampart, with sad eyes
    Watching the grey mists on the desolate plain
    Hover above the pools of stagnant rain—
A dreary landscape underneath drear skies:

---

* *La Pia* (de' Tolommei) is she who is mentioned in the 5th Canto of 'Il Purgatorio' as the bride of Nello della Pietra, and who was so cruelly imprisoned by the latter in a lonely fortress in the Maremma, where malaria erelong finished what grief had begun.

Along the mouldy battlements there lies
    His crimson banner, and close by are lain
    Fierce Nello's lances—cursed be his pain
Who caused her all these tears and weary sighs.

The stifling day is dead—dead as the fire
That in her heart flamed once with glad desire
    For him who wedded her one fatal day—
Death dwells in the Maremma, whose foul air
Insidious moves about her everywhere,
    Misty and cold and damp and drear and grey.

SONNETS ON THREE PAINTINGS BY BAZZI. (*Sodona*.)[9]

I. THE 'ST. SEBASTIAN' OF THE UFFIZII.

STILL young, still wonderful, august, and fair—
These long eventful ages that have fled
With changeful years where Arno's flood has sped
Through Tuscan dust until its sea-rest where
The Pisan waves wash in, have brought no air
    Of dim decay about thy lovely head;
    Death has not come although thy wounds have bled
So long; nor yet about thy body bare
Has Time enwrapt his dull and dubious hue:
With neck thrown back, and face, that fairer is
    Than ever man's was, lifted to the blue
Of heaven for all the summer winds to kiss
    And soothe thy deathly pain—what is the clue
Thine eyes have found, dreamful with mysteries?

II. 'CHRIST BEFORE THE SCOURGING.' (*Siena*.)

No lurid sky is here, thunder and rain
    Come from no heaven in wrath, no fierce men shake

Their spears before the sad strain'd eyes, or make
Their laughter shrilly mock his bygone reign:
Only the figure of a man in pain—
    Dire thirst of spirit that no hand will slake—
    A man who doth not fear, who doth not quake
Although he knows how agony can gain
The soul from its allegiance—for, far off,
    He sees beyond the cross, the grave, and death
        A multitude of ever nobler years—
What then to him the cruel jeer and scoff,
    What then to him although a few hours' breath
        Be spent in agony too great for tears?

III. On the Nineteenth Fresco of the St. Benedict Series on the Cloister-Walls of the Monastery of Monte Oliveto Maggiore. (*Umbria.*)

(*Come Florenzo manda male femmine al Monastero.*)

Wouldst thou indeed, St. Benedict, have stood
    Thus undismayed while this fair wanton band
    Came from the outer world, that joyous land
Long since condemned by thee; could thy calm mood
Have thus outlasted; would not strange thoughts brood
    Within that eager brain until thy hand
    Withstayed awhile the banishing command
And beckon'd rather for glad wine and food?

But if, Florenzo, curses dwelt with thee
    Because of tempted saints, at least we feel,
    As Bazzi did, a joyous rapture steal
Our sense away,—for like a dream is she
    Who, clothed in undulating azure folds,
    Still breathes the charm which over men she holds.

DURING MUSIC.

O TEARS that well up to my eyes,
    And vague thoughts wandering thro' my brain,
Whence come ye? From what alien skies,
    From what dim sorrow, what strange pain?

I hear old memories astir
    In dusky twilights of the past:
O voices telling me of her,
    My soul, whom now I know at last:

I know her not by any name,
    But she with hope or fear is pale;
I see her ere this body came
    From mortal womb with mortal wail.

Later and later through long years,
    Through generations of dead men,
I see her in her mist of tears,
    I see her in her shroud of pain.

I see her whom the æons have raised
    From one dim birth to endless life;
I see her strive, regain, re-fail
    Forever in the endless strife.

I see her, soul of man, and soul
    Of woman, and in many lands:
Her eyes are fixt on some far goal
    But she hath neither thrall nor bands.

On one day yet to come I see
    This body pale and cold and dead:
The spirit once again made free
    Hovers triumphant overhead.

Again, again, O endless day,
    I see her in new forms pace on,
And ever with her on the way
    Fair kindred souls in unison.

O wandering thoughts within my brain,
    O voices speaking low to me,
O music sweet with stingless pain,
    Bring clear the vision that I see!

O ecstasy of sound, O pain!
    Too sad my heart, too sad the tears
It bringeth to my eyes again,
    Too strange the hopes, too strange the fears.

OUTLINES.

I. Two Majesties. (*A picture by Gérôme.*)

UPON a vast grey barren block
    Of granite towering o'er the waste
    Of level sands a lion hath paced,
And now lies crouching: from the rock
He stares o'er leagues of deserts where
No object gleams through the clear air—
    While far away the cloudless sun
    In golden blaze his rest hath won.

II. Melancholia. (*Albrecht Dürer.*)

She sits, with symbols of the pride
    That Reason hath, about her strewn:
    Her lips move with no secret rune,
But on her forehead doth abide
Weariness of all things that be,

And from her eyes dreams Mystery.
Life she hath drunken to the dregs, and lo
She knows scarce more than children know.

III. Veronica Veronese. (*Dante Gabriel Rossetti.*)

She strikes the mystic chord, and on
Her face the low soft echo seems
To dwell: and in her eyes are dreams
That Love not yet hath stirr'd but shone
On only from afar, until
The hour come of his conquering will.
Fair spirit of woman and sweet sound—
Each seems with other interwound.

THE WATER-JOY.†

(*On the Lesse—Southern Belgium.*)

HERE at the river-bend, where stoop
The trailing willows on one side,
We drift by banks where, stretching wide,
A low rich meadow bears a troop
Of wilding flowers, moon-daisies white,
Tall meadow-sweet with blossoms light,
King-cups and purple scabious,
The snow-white chickweed, slim hare-bell,
The tiny scarlet pimpernel,
And trailing white convolvulus.

Fair as the fairest, on the stream
The Lesser water-lilies gleam
In starry masses far and near,
The joy of running waters clear.

---

† The *Frog-bit*, or Lesser Water-lily. *See* Note 10.

THE CRESCENT MOON.

AS though the Power that made the nautilus
A living glory o'er seas perilous
Scatheless to roam, had from the utmost deep
Called a vast flawless pearl from out its sleep
And carv'd it crescent wise, exceeding fair,—
So seems the crescent moon that thro' the air
　　With motionless motion glides from out the west,
　　And sailing onward ever seems at rest.

A DREAM.

LAST night thro' a haunted land I went,
Upon whose margins Ocean leant
　　Waveless and soundless save for sighs
That with the twilight airs were blent.

And passing, hearing never stir
Of footfall, or the startled whirr
　　Of birds, I said, 'In this land lies
Sleep's home, the secret haunt of her.'

And then I came upon a stone
Whereon these words were writ alone,
　　The soul who reads, its body dies
Far hence that moment without moan.

And then I knew that I was dead,
And that the shadow overhead
　　Was not the darkness of the skies
But that from which my soul had fled.

MORNING.

SEE, see, the sunlight breaking
    Over the mountain walls,
In golden shafts and streamers
    Adown their slopes it falls;
The curled white clouds are flushing,
The dim grey tarns are blushing,
And o'er the upland places
    The joyous cuckoo calls!

It steals adown the valleys,
    It takes the pine tops there,
And all the aery birches
    Wave now like golden hair;
O'er torrents wildly splashing
A myriad lights go flashing
And make a dazzling shimmer
    Within the spray-swept air.

With fiery crimson glowing
    Shine all the mountain walls;
Hark, the sweet noise like laughter
    Of a myriad waterfalls!
The curled white clouds are flushing,
The dim grey tarns are blushing
And o'er the upland places
    The joyous cuckoo calls!

OUTLINES.

I. SAPPHO.

THE high Leucadian steep aglow
　　With sunlight on its tinted side;
　　Dark blue, sky-bounded far and wide
The Attic ocean dreams below;
And on the highest craggy height
A woman stands in waving white:
　　'Tis she whose heart's name was Desire,
　　Who in the deep waves quenched its fire.

II. LAIS.

Within a marble balcony
　　She sits whom all of Greece called fair,
　　Lais of the wondrous golden hair:
Beyond her is the dimpled sea,
Beside her the wild fig-leaves twine
In shadow with the trailing vine:—
　　So fair without; within lie deep
　　The tigress-lusts that never sleep.

III. HYPATIA.

She stands within the lecture-room,—
　　A glory on her perfect face:
　　Perhaps some echo fills the place,
Some echo of the coming doom
When she, defiant still, will stand
With brave eyes scorning the foul band:
　　What care hath she of death—it means
　　The ruptured veil that true life screens.

93

NOTE.

'Australia has rightly been named the Land of the Dawning. Wrapped in the mist of early morning, her history looms vague and gigantic. The lonely horseman riding between the moonlight and the day sees vast shadows creeping across the shelterless and silent plains, hears strange noises in the primeval forest, where flourishes a vegetation long dead in other lands. . . . In Australia alone is to be found the Grotesque, the Weird, the strange scribblings of Nature learning how to write.'—MARCUS CLARKE.

AUSTRALIAN SKETCHES.

THE LAST ABORIGINAL.

I SEE him sit, wild-eyed, alone,
    Amidst gaunt, spectral, moonlit gums—
He waits for death: not once a moan
    From out his rigid fixt lips comes;
His lank hair falls adown a face
    Haggard as any wave-worn stone,
And in his eyes I dimly trace
The memory of a vanished race.

The lofty ancient gum-trees stand,
    Each grey and ghostly in the moon,
The giants of an old strange land
    That was exultant in its noon
When all our Europe was o'erturned
    With deluge and with shifting sand,
With earthquakes that the hills inurned
And central fires that fused and burned.

The moon moves slowly through the vast
    And solemn skies; the night is still,
Save when a warrigal springs past
    With dismal howl, or when the shrill
Scream of a parrot rings which feels
    A twining serpent's fangs fixt fast,
Or when a grey opossum squeals,
Or long iguana, as it steals

95

From bole to bole disturbs the leaves:
　　But hush'd and still he sits—who knows
That all is o'er for him who weaves
　　With inner speech, malign, morose,
A curse upon the whites who came
　　And gather'd up his race like sheaves
Of thin wheat, fit but for the flame—
Who shot or spurned them without shame.

He knows he shall not see again
　　The creeks whereby the lyre-birds sing—
He shall no more upon the plain,
　　Sun-scorch'd, and void of water-spring,
Watch the dark cassowaries sweep
　　In startled flight, or, with spear lain
In ready poise, glide, twist, and creep
Where the brown kangaroo doth leap.

No more in silent dawns he'll wait
　　By still lagoons, and mark the flight
Of black swans near: no more elate
　　Whirl high the boomerang aright
Upon some foe: he knows that now
　　He too must share his race's night—
He scarce can know the white man's plough
Will one day pass above his brow.

Last remnant of the Austral race
　　He sits and stares, with failing breath:
The shadow deepens on his face,
　　For 'midst the spectral gums waits death:
A dingo's sudden howl swells near—
　　He stares once with a startled gaze,
As half in wonder, half in fear,
Then sinks back on his unknown bier.

IN THE RANGES.

Through a dark cleft between two hills
A narrow passage leads the way
Close by a lonely lake; two rills,
Its children, sing the livelong day,
And from the water's lapping edge
The low tones of the long reeds come—
No other sound, save in the sedge
A black swan crooning; all the heights are dumb.

This cleft leads to an open space
Where arching tree-ferns grow around,
A still and solitary place:
Long waving grass grows from the ground,
And great green lizards half-awake
Lie silent hours, and in the light
The fiery glances of a stealthy snake
Keep glinting, glinting, like twin stars at night.

Beyond, a wooded gully lies—
A greenstone on the topaz plain;
In its deep shade no glaring skies
E'er shine, so thick are overlain
The branches of the ancient trees;
Within its depths the lyre-bird hides,
And, save at mid-noon, never cease
The bell-birds singing where the streamlet glides.

Far off on higher uplands grow
The spicy gum and hardy box,
The delicate acacias throw
Their feather-leafings o'er the rocks,
And grey-green misletoe doth creep
Till tree by tree is overlaid—

While in the noonday stillness sleep
The bright rosellas 'mid the wild-vine's shade.

Gippsland, Jan., 1878.

NOON-SILENCE. (*Australian Forest.*)

A lyre-bird sings a low melodious song—
Then all is still: a soft wind breathes along
The lofty gums and faintly dies away:
And Silence wakes and knows her dream is day.

THE STOCK-DRIVER'S RIDE.

O'er the range, and down the gully, across the river bed
We are riding on the tracks of the cattle that have fled:
The mopokes all are laughing and the cockatoos are
    screaming,
And bright amidst the stringy-barks the parrakeets are
    gleaming:

The wattle-blooms are fragrant, and the great magnolias fair
Make a heavy sleepy sweetness in the hazy morning air,
But the rattle and the crashing of our horses' hoofs ring out
And the cheery sound we answer with our long repeated
    shout—

Coo-ee-coo-ee-eee! Coo-ee-coo-eee—Coo-ee—Coo-ee!
'Damnation Dick' he hears us, and he shrills back Whoo-ee-
    ee!
'Damnation Dick' the prince of native trackers thus we call
From the way he swigs his liquor and the oaths that he can
    squall!

Thro' more ranges, thro' more gullies, down sun-scorched
    granite ways
We go crashing, slipping, thundering in our joyous morning
    race—
And the drowsy 'possums shriek and o'er each dried-up
    creek
The wallaroos run scuttling as if playing hide-and-seek:

And like iron striking iron do our horses' hoofs loud ring
As down the barren granite slopes we leap and slide and
    spring;
Then one range further only and we each a moment rein
Our steaming steeds as wide before us stretches out the
    grassy plain!

And 'Damnation Dick' comes running like a human
    kangaroo
And he cries the herd have bolted to the creek of Waharoo!
So we swing across the desert and for miles and miles we go
Till men and horses pant athirst i' the fierce sun's fiery glow.

And at last across the plains where the kangaroos fly leaping
And the startled emus in their flight go circularly sweeping,
We see the trees that hide the spring of Waharoo and there
The cattle all are standing still—the bulls with a fierce stare!

Then off to right goes Harry on his sorrel 'Pretty Jane,'
And to the left on 'Thunderbolt' Tom scours across the
    plain,
And Jim and I well-mounted and on foot 'Damnation Dick'
Go straight for Waharoo and our stockwhips fling and flick!

Ho there goes old 'Blackbeetle,' the patriarch of the herd!
His doughty courage vanish'd when Tom's long leash
    cracked and whirred,

And after him the whole lot flee and homeward head-long
   dash—
What bellowing flight and thunder of hoofs as thro' the
   scrub we crash!

Back through the gum-tree gullies, and over the river-bed,
And past the sassafras ranges whereover at dawn we sped,
With thunderous noise and shouting the drivers and driven
   flee—
And this was the race that was raced by Tom, Jim, Harry,
   and me!

THE DEATH OF THE LUBRA.‡

Stung by an adder unto death
   To this rough hut she comes to die:
All day the fierce noon's fiery breath
   Hath filled the blazing sky—

The long, strange, soundless Austral day
   Where through primeval forests come
No cry or song, and far away
   The bell-birds ev'n are dumb—

At sundown, tumult sweeps the skies
   From where a thousand parrots shrill;
The laughing-birds' terrific cries
   The rapid twilight fill.

And when the great moon rising gleams
   Athwart the rotting hut where low
The lubra bends, one cry she screams
   As though some unseen blow

‡ The native name for 'wife.'

Had stricken her with sudden might:—
Without, flits past the wailing owl,
And through the gloom of darkening night
Swells high the wild-dog's howl.

AUSTRALIAN TRANSCRIPTS.

I. AN ORANGE GROVE. (*Victoria*.)

THE short sweet purple twilight dreams
Of vanish'd day, of coming night;
And like gold moons in the soft light
Each scented drooping orange gleams
From out the glossy leaves black-green
That make through noon a cool dark screen.
The dusk is silence, save the thrill
That stirs it from cicalas shrill.

II. BLACK SWANS ON THE MURRAY LAGOONS.

The long lagoons lie white and still
Beneath the great round Austral moon:
The sudden dawn will waken soon
With many a delicious thrill:
Between this death and life the cries
Of black swans ring through silent skies—
And the long wash of the slow stream
Moves as in sleep some bodeful dream.

III. BREAKING BILLOWS AT SORRENTO. (*Victoria*.)

A sky of whirling flakes of foam,
A rushing world of dazzling blue:
One moment, the sky looms in view—
The next, a crash in its curv'd dome,

A tumult indescribable,
And eyes dazed with the miracle.
     Here breaks by circling day and night
     In thunder the sea's boundless might.

IV. SHEA-OAK TREES AN A STORMY DAY. (*S.E. Victoria.*)[11]

O'er sandy tracts the shea-oak trees
     Droop their long wavy grey-green trails:
     And inland wandering moans and wails
The long blast of the ocean-breeze:
Like loose strings of a viol or harp
These answering sound—now low, now sharp
     And keen, a melancholy strain:
     A death-song o'er the mournful plain.

V. MID-NOON IN JANUARY.

Upon a fibry fern-tree bough
     A huge iguana lies alow,
     Bright yellow in the noonday glow
With bars of black,—it watcheth now
A gorgeous insect hover high
Till suddenly its lance doth fly
     And catch the prey—but still no sound
     Breathes 'mid the green fern-spaces round.

VI. IN THE FERN. (*Gippsland.*)

The feathery fern-trees make a screen
     Wherethrough the sun-glare cannot pass—
     Fern, gum, and lofty sassafras:
The fronds sweep over, palely green,
And underneath are orchids curl'd
Adream through this cool shadow-world;
     A fragrant greenness—like the noon
     Of lime-trees in an English June.

102

VII. SUNSET AMID THE BUFFALO MOUNTAINS. (*N.E. Victoria.*)[12]

Across the boulder'd majesty
    Of the great hills the passing day
    Drifts like a wind-borne cloud away
Far off beyond the western sky:
And while a purple glory spreads,
With straits of gold and brilliant reds,
    An azure veil, translucent, strange,
    Dreamlike steals over each dim range.

VIII. THE FLYING MOUSE. (*New South Wales—Moonlight.*)[13]

The eucalyptus-blooms are sweet
    With honey, and the birds all day
    Sip the clear juices forth: brown-grey,
A bird-like thing with tiny feet
Cleaves to the boughs, or with small wings
Amidst the leafy spaces springs,
    And in the moonshine with shrill cries
    Flits batlike where the white gums rise.

IX. THE WOOD-SWALLOWS. (*Sunrise.*)§

The lightning-stricken giant gum
    Stands leafless, dead—a giant still
    But heedless of this sunrise-thrill:
What stir is this where all was dumb?—
What seem like old dead leaves break swift,
And lo, a hundred wings uplift
    A cloud of birds that to and fro
    Dart joyous midst the sunrise-glow.

---

§ The wood-swallows of Australia have the singular habit of clustering like bees or bats on the boughs of a dead tree.

X. THE BELL-BIRD.

The stillness of the Austral noon
    Is broken by no single sound—
    No lizards even on the ground
Rustle amongst dry leaves—no tune
The lyre-bird sings—yet hush! I hear
A soft bell tolling, silvery clear!
    Low soft aerial chimes, unknown
    Save 'mid these silences alone.

XI. THE ROCK-LILY. (*New South Wales.*)[14]

The amber-tinted level sands
    Unbroken stretch for leagues away
    Beyond these granite slabs, dull grey
And lifeless, herbless—save where stands
The mighty rock-flow'r towering high,
With carmine blooms crowned gloriously:
    A giant amongst flowers it reigns,
    The glory of these Austral plains.

XII. THE FLAME-TREE. (*New South Wales.*)[15]

For miles the Illawarra range
    Runs level with Pacific seas:
    What glory when the morning breeze
Upon its slopes doth shift and change
Deep pink and crimson hues, till all
The leagues-long distance seems a wall
    Of swift uncurling flames of fire
    That wander not nor reach up higher.

MORNING IN THE BUSH (*December.*)

The magpie midst the wattle-blooms
    Is singing loud and long:
What fragrance in the scatter'd scent,
    What magic in the song!
On yonder gum a mopoke's throat
    Out-gurgles laughter grim,
And far within the fern-tree scrub
    A lyre-bird sings his hymn.
Amongst the stringy-barks a crowd
    Of dazzling parrakeets—
But high o'er all the magpie loud
    His joyous song repeats.

JUSTICE. (*Uncivilized and Civilized.*)

Ling-Tso Ah Sin, on Murderer's Flat
One morning caught an old grey rat:
'Ah, white man, I have got you now!
But no—dust be upon my brow
If needless blood I cause to fall—
So go, there's world-room for us all!'

That night Ah Sin was somehow shot—
By *accident*! For he had got
From earth a little gold—black sin
For *thee*, though not for us, Ah Sin!

Murderer's Flat, Feb., 1878.

105

THE COROBBOREE. (*Midnight.*)

Deep in the forest-depths the tribe
    A mighty blazing fire have made:
Round this they spring with frantic yells
    In hideous pigments all arrayed—

One barred with yellow ochre, one
    A skeleton in startling white,
There one who dances furiously
    Blood-red against the great fire's light,—

With death's insignia on his breast,
    In rude design, the swart chief springs;
And loud and long each echoes back
    The savage war-cry that he sings.

Within the forest dark and dim
    The startled cockatoos like ghosts
Flit to and fro, the mopokes scream,
    And parrots rise in chattering hosts;

The gins and lubras crouch and watch
    With eager shining brute-like eyes,
And ever and again shrill back
    Wild echoes of the frantic cries:—

Like some infernal scene it is—
    The forest dark, the blazing fire,
The ghostly birds, the dancing fiends,
    Whose savage chant swells ever higher.

Afar away gaunt wild-dogs howl,
    And strange cries vaguely call: but white
The placid moon sails on, and flame
    The silent stars above the night.

MOONRISE SKETCHES.

I. MOONRISE AT SEA.

THE long slow swell of the still sea
Rises and falls, and sluggishly
The wind-bound ship rolls to and fro,
Soundless, save when the huge sails go
With a heavy boom from left to right:
A few stars only trail their light
In quivering snaky gleams below
In the sea's depths, as though from caves
Within whose twilight glooms no waves
Move ever serpents writhe and rise:
But westward far where sea and skies
Blend in one darkness breaks a beam
Of wan faint light—and now a gleam
Curv'd like a golden scimetar
And bright as though welded from a star
Hangs for a moment, grows and grows
More round and large, a golden rose
Of one immaculate petal made:
And now the moon is risen, has laid
The music of her magic smile
Upon the dim dark seas till mile
On mile, league upon league, are bright
With a broad track of silver light,
And all the ship's sails seem to be
Of moonbeam-gossamer woven free.

II. MOONRISE IN AUSTRALIA.

A trackless forest all around
Of lofty gums that from the ground
As saplings sprang in ages past:—
The short sweet twilight fadeth fast
And from the forest depths I hear
The locust's whirling noise, the clear
Soft magpie song, the sudden scream
Where cockatoos like white ghosts gleam
Among the melancholy boughs,
The wild-dog's bark from where there browse
Stray herds of kangaroos, the cry
Of something death-struck—as I lie
And listen to these sounds I see
Long moonbeams pierce a lofty tree
Like random lances thrust to kill
Some fiend who baffles all their skill;
And even as with sleepy eyes
I watch, the full moon through the skies
Sails with a seeming moveless motion,
A globe of fire in a purple ocean.

III. MOONRISE FROM IONA, N.B.

Here, where in dim forgotten days
A savage people chanted lays
To long since perished gods, I stand:
The sea breaks in, runs up the sand,
Retreats as with a long-drawn sigh,
Sweeps in again; again leaves dry
The ancient beach, so old and yet
S0 new that as the strong tides fret
The island barriers in their flow

The ebb-hours of each day can know
A surface change. The day is dead,
The sun is set, and overhead
The white north stars shine keen and bright;
The wind upon the sea is light
And just enough to stir the deep
With phosphorescent gleams and sweep
The spray from salt waves as they rise:
And yonder light—is't from the skies,
Some meteor strange, a burning star—
Or a lamp hung upon a spar
Of vessel undescried? It gleams
And rises slowly, till it seems
A burning isle, an angel-throne
Reset on earth, a mountain-cone
Of gold new-risen from sea-caves—
Until at last above the waves,
Salt with Atlantic brine, it swims
A silver crescent, Now no hymns
In the wild Runic speech are heard,
No chant, no sacrificial word:
But only moans the weary sea,
And only the cold wind sings free,
And where the Runic temples stood
The bat flies and the owl doth brood.

IV. MOONRISE ON THE VENETIAN LAGOONS.

A more than twilight darkness dwells
Upon the long lagoons: the bells
Of distant Venice come and go
Like sounds in dreams; the tide's soft flow
Sweeps onward, and a wandering gull
Flits o'er the track of yon black hull
Just fading in the gloom—no more

I see or hear 'tween shore and shore:
But as I lie and dreamily
Watch the dark water from the sea
Slip past the boat, in its blurred sky
I see the crescent moon on high
Casting curv'd golden flakes far down
Amidst the calm lagoon—a crown
Broken innumerably up,
The gold bands of a broken cup.
I take an oar and make a rift
In the soft tide of the lagoons,—
And lo, the blade itself doth lift
A score of quivering crescent moons,
And as they flash I seem to see
Each droplet with a small moon flee.

V. MOONRISE ON THE ANTARCTIC.

The huge white icebergs silently
Voyage with us through this lonely sea,
Noiseless and lifeless, yet they seem
Like haunted islands in a dream
Holding strange secrets that no one
May know and live. In the bright sun
They shine immeasurably fair,
Bluer than bluest summer air,
Or clear to the very heart with green
Pure light, or amethyst as seen
'Mid sunset-clouds—but now they shine
With a cold gleam and have no sign
Of loveliness. The ship swings on,
Plunging mid surging seas whereon
Few vessels ever sail, and as
Slowly the long hours come and pass
The late moon rises cold and white,

And sends a flood of wintry light
Along the sweeping waves and round
Our black and sea-worn hull. A sound
Far off dies while it grows—some seal
Long-drifted, frozen, waking but to feel
Death's grip. And now the spectral isles
Grow whiter, icier still, and seem
More hollow, with a strange weird gleam
As though some pale unreal fires
Consumed them to their utmost spires
Yet without flame or heat. And still
The moon doth rise, and seems to fill
Each berg anew with life: we sail.
Upon a strange sad sea, where pale
And moonshine isles float all around,
Voyaging onward without sound.

THE SHADOWED SOULS.

If the soul withdraweth from the body, what profit thereafter hath a man of all the days of his life?

SHE died indeed, but to him her breath
Was more than a light blown out by death:
He knew that they breathed the self-same air,
That not midst the dead was her pale face fair
But that she waited for him somewhere.

To some dead city, or ancient town,
Where the mould'ring towers were crumbling down,
Or in some old mansion habited
By dust and silence and things long dead,
He knew the Shadows of Souls were led.

For years he wandered a weary way,
His eyes shone sadder, his hair grew grey:
But still he knew that she lived for whom
No grave lay waiting, no white carv'd tomb,
No earthy silence, no voiceless gloom.

But once in a bitter year he came
To an old dying town with a long dead name
That eve, as he walked thro' the dusty ways
And the echoes woke in the empty place,
He came on a Shadow face to face.

It looked, but uttered no word at all
Then beckoned him into an old dim hall:
And lo, as soon as he passed between

112

The pillars with age and damp mould green
His eyes were dazed by a strange wild scene.

A thousand lamps fill'd the place with light,
And fountains glimmered faerily bright;
But never a single sound was heard,
The dreadful silence was never stirred,
Not even the breath of a single word

Came from the shadowy multitude,
More dense than the leaves in a summer wood,
Than the sands where the swift tides ebb and flow;
But ever the Shades moved to and fro
As windless waves on the sea will go.

Then he who had come to Shadow-land
Swift strode past many a group and band;
But never a glimpse he caught of her,
In fleeting shadow or loiterer,
For whom the earth held no sepulchre.

He knew that she was not dead whom he
So loved with bitterest memory,
To whom through anguish'd years he had prayed;
Yet came she never, no sign was made,
No touch on his haggard frame was laid.

At last to an empty room he came,
And there he saw in letters of flame—
'This is that palace no king controls,
A place unwritten in human scrolls—
This is the Haunt of Shadowed Souls:

'If thy Shadow-soul be here no more
Seek thine old life's deserted shore:
And there, mayhap, thou wilt find again,

Recovered now through sorrow and pain,
The Soul thou didst thy most to have slain.'

SLEEPY HOLLOW.**

(*In Memoriam: Ralph Waldo Emerson.*)

HE sleeps here the untroubled sleep
    Who could not bear the noise and moil
    Of public life, but far from toil
A happy reticence did keep

With Nature only open, free:
    Close by there rests the magic mind
    Of him who took life's thread to wind
And weave some poor soul's mystery

Of spirit-life, and make it live
    A type and wonder for all days;
    No sweeter soul e'er trod earth's ways
Than he who here at last did give

His body back to earth again.
    And now at length beside them lies
    One great and true and nobly wise,—
A King of Thought, whose spotless reign

The overwhelming years that come
    And drown the trash and dross and slime
    Shall keep a record of till Time
Shall cease, and voice of man be dumb.

** In Sleepy Hollow Cemetery are the graves of Thoreau and Hawthorne (to whom respectively reference is made in the first three verses) and near them, about two years ago, were laid the remains of Emerson.

114

At last he rests, whose high clear hope
    Was wont on lofty wings to scan
    The future destinies of man—
Who saw the Race through darkness grope,

Through mists and error, till at last
    The looked-for light, the longed-for age
    Should dawn for peasant, prince, and sage,
And centuries of night be past.

Thy rest is won: O loyal, brave,
    Wise soul, thy spirit is not dead—
    Thy wing'd words far and wide have fled,
Undying, they shall find no grave.

BIRCHINGTON REVISITED.

(D. G. R.)

HE sleeps a quiet sleep at last
    Who wearied for such blissful hours:
The stress of high-strung life is past,
The veil of death is o'er him cast,
    And for him hence no dark sky lowers.

Sweet is the air here, clear and sweet;
    The larks with jubilant voices sing,
And still their songs re-sing, repeat;
The grass, starr'd white with marguerite,
    Is yet memorious of Spring.

Yonder the blue sea, windless, still,
    Meets the blue sky-line far away—
Soundless, save when the wavelets spill
Their little crowns of foam, and fill
    The rock-pools full with swirling spray.

How sweet to rest here, and to know
    The silence and the utter peace!
To lie and rest and sleep below
While far away tired millions go
    With eyes all yearning for such ease.

'Tis better thus: alone, yet safe
    From night and day, from day and night;
Not here can jarring discords chafe
Thy soul too sensitive, or waif
    Of stinging envy blown from spite.

'Tis quiet here, and more than all
    Things else is rest a boon to thee—
Rest, peace, and sleep: above, the pall
    Of heaven; and past the white cliff-wall
    The ceaseless mystery of the sea.

JUNE'S ADVENT.

JUNE, wandering hence, smiles through the summer heat
In answer to the beckoning hand of May,
    Who, lily-crown'd, flits deck'd in green array
Through field and wood, and with her presence sweet
Fills all the birds with joy, and 'neath her feet
    Leaves fragrant flowers about each hedge-girt way:
    Laughing she chides sweet June for his delay—
Her rose-crown'd lover, whom she longs to meet.

Behold he comes, with splendour on his brow,
    All summer in his dark-blue dreamful eyes,
    And lips that move with murmurs of sweet song—
And lo, each recognising forest-bough
    Waves joyous welcome, and with eager cries
    Him thrushes greet with music loud and long.

PHANTASY.

RIDING o'er a lonely plain
  I came unto a wood—
  And there I met, in dreamful mood,
A damsel singing a low strain,
All ye who love me love in vain!

Her song it seemed far away,
  But oh her kiss was sweet:
  She led me to some green retreat,
And there within her arms I lay
The livelong day.

All ye who love me love in vain—
  I kissed her wistful face
  But found a leaf-strewn space
Alone, and far I heard her strain,
All ye who love me love in vain.

I seek the wood in twilit hours—
  At times I hear her sing:
  At times her white arms round me cling:
She leads me into magic bow'rs
And sings and wreathes me wilding flow'rs.

Her eyes are tears, and pain
  Is in her kiss, but wildly gay
  She laughs, and fades away,
And through the dim wood floats the strain,
All ye who love me love in vain.

QUINCE BLOSSOMS.

(To V. H. M. B.)

HOW delicately sweet and rare
These blossoms that the Roman air
   Hath nurtured exquisitely well:
A mighty branch! How late it knew
The fresh warm winds that round it blew
   Where high its parent tree did dwell.

And now within your room they make
A sweetness, as when lilies take
   The gloom from willow-darken'd streams:
Here Spring lies captive, where no wind
With furtive breath its blooms shall find
   Nor mock each transient blossom's dreams.

Love, Poetry, and Art are flow'rs
Sweet as the quince, and fill life's hours
   With joy and fragrance even as these:
Thrice happy thou that these three hast,
Sweet deathless flow'rs that aye will last
   Though quince-blooms wither on their trees.

ROME, *April*, 1883.

MAY-DAY.

(Castello del' Quattro Torre—near Siena.)

ABOVE, the Four Towers feel the wind
   With half-closed pinions rest and play
   Around the bastions old and grey—
But o'er the olive-slopes behind

It sweeps like some aerial stream,
Till every leaflet seems a gleam
    Of silver and the grasses sway
    In light and shade for miles away.

Around, the flowering wild-beans make
    A fresh Spring fragrance in the air:
    The crimson clover everywhere
Tempts the brown bees, and poppies shake
Their dust amongst the corn and stand
Like flames all over the green land—
    And in the sunlight's golden glare
    The snow-white lilies seem more fair.

The swallows sweep in endless flight
    Above the orchard-slopes below,
    White with the scented blossom-snow:
And hark! from yonder tree-clad height
The sweet voice of the Spring rings clear—
The herald Cuckoo, ever dear:
    And 'midst the warmth, the peace, the glow,
    The birthday of sweet May I know.

IN THE VAL MUGNONE.

(TO A. M. F. R. AND V. P.)

SPRING'S laughter rings down thro' the valley;
    A thousand sweet blossoms are there;
The world hath grown young and is happy
    And heedless of care.

The river flows dashing and splashing
    Past banks where the primroses blow;
The sunlight is streaming and flashing
    Where white olives grow.

Joy beats through the heart of the valley:
    A thrush sings loudly and long:
With the flow'rs and the birds we are happy,
    And life is a song.

IN MAREMMA.

THE ardent azure sky above—
Cloudless save little snowy isles
That without motion seem to move
So silently they sail through miles
Of that calm blue of upper sea,
White shoreless isles, unstable, free—

Around, an ocean of green grass,
Leagues upon leagues of rolling ground
That stretch unbroken till they pass
From sight in one long swelling mound
That fades indefinitely away
Into the sky-line's hazy grey.

Far north a rugged mountain-chain
Seems like a soft indefinite band
Against the deeper blue; a plain
Sweeps thence south-westward till the sand
That drifts about the Latin shore
Its sterile verdure covers o'er—

A plain where marshy waters meet
Drear pestilential tracts, where ring
No human voices, though the sweet
Song of the lark is trilled through Spring,
And myriad scented flowers unfold
And bloom above the treacherous mould.

At times a lonely horseman rides
Across the waste on shaggy steed;
There too the hunted brigand hides;
And often, with swift reckless speed,
The fierce wild-cattle snort and fly,
Tameless with savage liberty.

A SUNSET.
(*From the Gates of Volterra.*)

ABOVE the rugged Apennines
In long thick wavy purple lines
The storm-clouds rest: a space doth lie
Betwixt them, and here glares an eye
Socketless, blood-red, terrible.
Slowly the fire-globe sinks,—but as
Some miracle were come to pass,
Some ominous enchantic spell,—
Through the dark cloud-mass lying below
A sword of lurid red doth crawl
From whose serrated edges fall
Great blood-like clots—as if some woe
Impended where Volterra hung
Where the last gleams of day were flung.

ON THE CAMPAGNA.

I.

A LARK high in the heavens,
    A wilderness of grass—
White cloudlets trailing slowly
    Blue shadows as they pass—
Songs, flowers, and windy spaces
    Of skies divinely clear—

If Heaven is anywhere
'Tis surely here!

II.

The white moon leads the planets,
  Stars fill the skies—
But where the flow'rs are sleeping
  Grey mists arise—
The poison-mists are drifting,
  As o'er a shallow mere:
If death lurks anywhere
  'Tis surely here.

FIREFLIES. (*In the Cascine: Florence.*)

UNDER the olive-boughs and o'er
  The long lush grass the fireflies wheel
  In lonely flight, or rise and reel
In a strange mazy dance before
Yon ancient ilex that can keep
A darkness where no moonbeams creep:
  Like souls they seem that have no rest,
  With death-lights seeking still life's quest.

IN THE OLD PROTESTANT CEMETERY AT FLORENCE.

(*Easter*, 1883.)

THE light wind scarcely breathes between
  The close-set cypress boughs, nor stirs
To varying shades the ilex-green;
  A blackbird calls, a song-thrush whirrs
Through leafy dusk till somewhere near
Again its sweet wild song swells clear:—

But otherwise no sound to break
    The hallowed peace that broods where lies
The dust of her†† for whose sweet sake
    Firenze and its ardent skies
To all who love her sweet song-lore
Are dear and sacred evermore.

The river that she loved flows nigh,
    Slow washing to the Pisan sea—
Behind, where solemn hills slope high
    The Vallombrosan torrents flee
'Mid crags and pines—and yonder way
Morello and Fiesole.

The Tuscan spring is warm and bright
    As when she loved to watch the sun
Turn olive-leaves to slips of light,
    As fair the flowers where children run
And laugh amidst their childish pranks
Upon grey-green Mugnone's banks:

But quiet the urgent heart, the brain
    That wrought with ceaseless love and care
Sweet songs compact of joy and pain,
    Dreams from a soul that knew no air
Of common earth—now where songs are
The breath of souls she dwells afar.

And as I think of her my heart
    Turns back to last year's Easter-tide,‡‡
Remembering with a sudden smart;
    I see again the cliffs beside
The broad blue sea, in crescent bent
Half round the windy breast of Kent—

†† E. B. B., obiit 1861.
‡‡ D. G. R., obiit Easter, 1882.

I see the little graveyard lie,
  The tombs encrusted with sea-salt;
Above, I hear the larks sing high
  Within the cloud-flecked azure-vault—
And surely that sound from the deep
Must soothe those sleeping their long sleep.

He too has rest, and knows no more
  Of joy or pain: and as the sea
Is secret, so for evermore
  His voice is hushed. The mystery
Of song! But no, afar he sings,
Afar he knows diviner springs,

Afar he feels the mystic change
  That veiled death wrought,—or here again
His new-framed soul doth upward range
  Preparing for a nobler strain:
The joy of Death! that leaves us here
To live anew, or to some sphere

Beyond the earth and mortal woes
  Wafts spirits to some stellar bliss!
Ev'n as a flower from winter's throes
  Is born to feel Spring's breathless kiss,
So is he filled with joy who here
Wept oft to find life barren, drear.

A RECORD.

(A FRAGMENT.)

I HEAR the dark tempestuous sea
Boom through the night monotonously,
The hoarse faint cries of breaking waves
Lashed by the wind that moans and raves
Upon the deep—I hear them fall
Against cliff-bases smooth and tall,
A music wild, funereal.

I seem to listen to a sound
That circles earth for ever round,
The dirge of an eternal song,
A dull deep music swept along
The listening coasts of many lands,
Sighed mournfully o'er level sands,
Or thunder'd amidst rocky strands.

I sit within my lonely room
Where the lamp's flame just breaks the gloom,
And thro' the darkness of the night
I see far down a starry light
Where nestled safely in the chine
The village street in one long line
Doth like a glittering serpent shine.

The keen wind blows through the dark skies,
The stars look down like countless eyes
That see and know, and therefore stare
Unmoved 'midst their serene high air:

And life seems but a dream, a shade
Which fleeing Time o'er space hath laid,
But which with Time shall one day fade.

Old memories are mine once more,
I see strange lives I lived of yore;
With dimm'd sight see I far off things,
I feel the breath of bygone springs,
And ringing strangely in mine ears
I hear old laughter, alien tears
Slow falling, voices of past years.

Far back the soul can never see—
But dreams restore mysteriously
Dim visions of a possible past,
A time ere the last bond was cast
Aside that bound the struggling soul
Unto the brute, and first some goal
Loomed dimly over Life's vast shoal.

And dreaming so I live my dream:
I see a yellow turbid stream
Heavily flowing thro' clustered weeds
Of tropic growth, and 'midst the reeds
Of tall green rice upon its bank
A crouching tiger, long and lank,
With slow tail swaying from flank to flank:

Its eyes are yellow flames, and burn
Upon a man who dips an urn
Into the Ganges' sacred wave,
Unknowing he has reached his grave—
A short hoarse roar, a scream, a blow!
And even as I shudder, lo
My tiger-self I seem to know.

And dreaming so I live my dream:
I see a sunrise-glory gleam
Against vast mountain-heights, and there
Upon a peak, precipitous, bare,
I see an eagle scan the plain
Immeasurable of his domain,
With fierce untameable disdain:

When first the stars wax pale, his eyes
Front the wide east where day doth rise,
And with unflinching gaze look straight
Against the sun, then proud, elate,
On tireless wings he swoops on high
O'er countless leagues, and thro' the sky
Drifts like a dark cloud ominously:

Then as day dies and swift night springs.
I hear the sudden rush of wings
And see the eagle from the plain
Sweep to his eyrie once again
With fierce keen dauntless eyes aglow—
And even as I watch them, lo
Mine eagle-self I seem to know.

And dreaming so I live my dream:
I hear a savage voice, a scream
Scarcely articulate, and far
I see a red light like a star
Flash 'neath old trees, and the first fire
Made by the brutish tribe burn higher
Until unfed its flames expire:

I see the savage whose hand drew
The fire from wood, whose swift breath blew
The flame until it gained new strength,—
I see him stand supreme at length,

And pointing to the burning flame
Bend low his swart and trembling frame
And cry aloud a guttural name:

A god at last the tribe hath found,
A god at whose strange crackling sound
Each man must bend in dread until
This strange new god hath worked his will:
But lo, one day the fire spreads fast,
And ere its fury is o'erpast
The tribe within its furnace-blast

Hath perish'd, save one man alone
Who far in sudden fear hath flown:
But with a gleam of new-born thought
A second flame he soon hath wrought
Only to tramp it down, aware
At last that no dead god lies there,
Or one for whom no man need care.

He looks around to see some god,
And far upon the fire-scorch'd sod
He sees his brown burnt tribesmen lie,
And thinks their voices fill the sky,
And dreads some unseen sudden blow—
And even as I watch him, lo
My savage-self I seem to know.

And dreaming so I live my dream:
I see a flood of moonlight gleam
Between vast ancient oaks, and round
A rough-hewn altar on the ground
Weird Druid priests are gathered
While through their midst a man is led
With face that seems already dead:

A low chant swells throughout the wood,
Then comes a solemn interlude
Ere loudlier rings dim aisles along
Some ancient sacrificial song;
Before the fane the victim kneels,
And without sound he forward reels
When the priest's knife the death-blow deals:

The moonlight falls upon his face,
His blood is spatter'd o'er the place,
But now he is ev'n as a flow'r
Uprooted in some tempest hour,
Dead, but whose seed shall elsewhere grow:
And as I look upon him, lo
Some old ancestral self I know.

Thus far dreams bring mysteriously
Visions of past lives back to me;
Visions alone perhaps they are,
Each one a wandering futile star
Flash'd o'er the mental firmament,—
Yet may be thus in past times went
My soul in gradual ascent.

None sees the slow sure upward sweep
By which the soul from life-depths deep
Ascends—unless, mayhap, when free
With each new death we backward see
The long perspective of our race,
Our multitudinous past lives trace
Since first as breath of God through space

Each came, and filled the lowest thing
With life's faint pulse scarce quivering;
So ever onward upward grew,
And ever with each death-birth knew

An old sphere left, a mystic change—
A sense of exultation strange
Thus through a myriad lives to range.

But even in our mortal lives
At times the eager spirit strives
To gain through subtle memories
Some hint of life's past mysteries—
Brief moments they, that flash before
Bewilder'd eyes some scene of yore,
Some vivid hour returned once more.

Swift through the darken'd clouds of sense
A sudden lightning-gleam intense
Reveals some glimpse of the long past,
Some memory comes back at last—
And yet 'twas but a sudden strain
Of song—a scent—a sound of rain—
Some trifle—made all clear again.

With a swift flash such glimpses come
And go—but there are times for some
When keen the vision is, so keen
That thenceforth the indelible scene
Remains within the mind for aye,
Some reminiscence sad or gay,
Some action of a bygone day.

Thus came to me memorious gleams
From the closed past, no sleep-brought dreams
But revelations flashed out swift
Upon the mind: a sudden lift
Of the dense cloud of all past years,—
A moment when the thrilling ears
Heard, or the eyes slow filled with tears.

Thus hath there flashed across my sight
A desert in a blinding light
Of scorching sun, a dreary waste
Of burning sand where seldom paced
The swift gaunt camels with their freight
Of merchandise, but where the weight
Of silence lay inviolate.

There a few sterile rocks lay white
In the sun's glare, a band by might
Of old convulsion thither hurled
In the far days of the young world:
And in their midst a hollow cave
Was cleft, where dwelt, as in a grave,
One who came thence his soul to save.

Young, and from out the joyous strife
Of men he came to this drear life:
No more for him the wine's swift spell,
No more for him love's miracle—
But bitter as the dead sea dust
Seem'd all past joys,—dread things to thrust
Aside, all equally accursed.

In fervid prayer all day he sought
God's grace: in dreams at night he fought
The fierce temptations born of youth:
Awake, he strove to reach God's truth—
Asleep, he felt his passions rise
And darken all the heav'nly skies
With dread deceitful lovely lies.

Thus year by year he fell and rose
In endless conflict, till his woes
Fill'd all his days with burning tears
And dreadful never-ending fears:

Haggard he grew from scanty food,
With sun and blast and shelter rude
And terrors of his lonelihood.

With long hair streaming out behind
He raced before the burning wind,
With wild insane strained eyes alert
For demons lurking to his hurt—
And though the sun beat fiercely hot
Upon the sands, he heeded not
But like a wand'ring shadow shot

Across the burning level waste,
Oft shouting as he wildly raced
'My body is in hell, but I,
Its soul, thus hither speed and cry
To God to blow me as a leaf
From out this agony of grief,
To slay, and give me death's relief!'

Oft as he fled, with from his mouth
The white froth blown thro' maddening drouth,
He pass'd the crouching lion's lair—
But when his shrill laugh fill'd the air
The desert monarch shrank, as though
He feared this raving shadow's woe,
This haggard wretch with eyes aglow.

But when the sun sank past the west
The hermit fled the desert, lest
God's eyes should lose him in the night,
And foes Satanic guide his flight
Till soul and body once again
Made one should with the pangs of twain
In hell for ever writhe in pain.

But when sleep came to him he lay
In peace, and oft a smile would play
Upon his face as though once more
In dreams he lived his life of yore,—
The life he did himself dismiss,
The old sweet time of joy and bliss,—
Heard laughter, or felt some loved kiss.

Thus have I seen, and seeing known
That he who lived afar alone,
A hermit on a dreary waste,
Was even that soul mine eyes have traced
Through brute and savage steadily,
That he even now is part of me
Just as a wave is of the sea.

Far out across the deep doth swell
The hoarse boom of the Black-Rock bell,
A heavy moan monotonous,
An inner sea-sound ominous
As though throughout the ocean there
Relentless Conscience aye did bear
A bitter message of despair.

Still sweeps the old impetuous sea
Around the green earth ceaselessly—
Changeless, yet full of change, it seems
The very mirror of those dreams
We call men's lives—for are not they
Like life-sea waves Fate's wind doth sway
And break, yet which pass not away

Through depths of silent air, but blend
Once more with the great deep and lend
Their never dying music sweet
To the great choral song complete;

Each death is but a birth, a change—
Each soul through myriad byeways strange,
Through birth and death, doth upward range.

RAINBOW SKETCHES.

I. THE RAINBOW.

THE rain-clouds slowly trail from the dun hills
   And the grey mists retreat from the grey seas,
   And a fresh wind comes forth and shakes the trees
And blows the foam from the o'er-flooded rills,

And softly then the sun the wet sky fills
   With chastened lights, and a long shimmer flees
   From cloud to cloud till over the drench'd leas
A Rainbow curves its arc and glows and thrills.

II. TOWARDS SUNSET. (*Western Islands, N.B.*)

The whole sky to the west is wild
With storm and tempest; clouds are piled
Mass upon mass, like mountain-heights
In skyey regions far; strange lights

Gleam o'er their hollow flanks as though
The furious wind that rears them so
Breath'd fiery breaths—and overhead
A maze of flying mists is spread,
Cloud, mist, and rain, pure dazzling white
A moment, lurid next and bright
In slaty black, and now dull grey
Descending in broad sheets away
In furious rain above the sea.

Far in the west shines yellowly
A widening cloud-strait, and thereby
The sun descending leaves the sky
With ominous gleams—crimson flames,
Purple, and bronze, hues without names;
And ever underneath toils wide
The windy sea, with wave and tide
Lashing each other into flying
Foam. Now, just as day is dying,
The storm-clouds with a sudden thrill
Seem windless and grow strangely still,
And almost doth it seem as though
Yon fugitive soft lights that glow
Are the dying storm's dying smiles
Dreamily waving to and fro,
Like mists of the Enchanted Isles:
Still wavering they blend and rise
Till perfectly they arch the skies

In one vast crescent bow, far seen
O'er land and sea—an arch of green
And soft and shadowy amethyst,
Crimson as pure as sunrise-mist,
Azure æthereally blue,
And yellow gold with opal hue:—
Some moments thus it flawless stands,
A sign, a glory o'er the lands—
The Soul of Hope it is we see
Cloth'd in her immortality.

III. DRIFTING RAIN-LIGHTS.

Around this lonely sea-loch stand
Huge mountain-shapes, a giant band
Dwelling in solitude for aye,

And silent save when through the grey
Chill skies the eagle screams, or down
Some sheer abyss where shadows frown
In noontide loosen'd boulders fall
Whirling and crashing, until all
Is still once more, and once again
The mountain-silence broods in pain.

A curdling fume beyond the reach
Of yonder headland, where the beach
Scarce slopes a yard, betrays the tide's
Fierce struggle where the current glides
With swiftly outward flow, and as
The conquering tide-waves inward pass
The sleeping wind unfolds its wings
And with sweet sudden laughter springs
Upon the loch and sweeps the spray
From startled wavelets fleeing away,
Whence wheeling to the slopes it flies
And where the heavy white mist lies
Strikes with dividing pinions till
The furtive sunlight on each hill
Gleams, and the toiling vapours curl
From crag to crag and wreathing whirl
To higher mountain-hollows where
Gaunt larches cling 'mid boulders bare.

And as the grey clouds slowly lift,
The sudden shimmering rain-lights drift
Hither and thither, flash and fly
As though bright spirits fill'd the sky—
Wings here of azure, there of red,
A golden glory overhead,
A sudden rosy glow, a streak
Of purple over some grey peak,
A lovely waft of green (as though

Some laughing sky-sprite from below
Had filch'd a sea-wave's hue), a gleam
Of amber like a strayed moon-beam,
A sudden joyous skyey revel
O'er mountain heights and lowland level,
Now forming to an arch, again
Flashing in drifting sprays of rain—
Fair phantom hues that pass away
Blown on the breath of dying day.

IV. THE CIRCLE OF ULLOA.[16]

The white mists swathe the mountain-flanks
And shroud the melancholy ranks
Of gaunt green pines, until these seem
Like ghostly figures in a dream
Each standing silent by his grave.
Far off swift mountain torrents rave
Down rugged gorges, and below—
Half muffled by the wastes of snow—
A cataract in thunder booms.
No sunlight fills these twilit glooms
But only a wan greyness drear,
And only where the peaks rise sheer
Above the pine-clad heights the sun
Faint yellow shines—a dismal gleam,
No flashing golden coloured stream.

But in the west a quiver stirs,
As though a wind amidst the firs
Were waving slow tired wings ere swift
Awakening it rose to drift
From hill to dale, from dale to hill,
And the long waving pine-boughs fill
With sudden music wild and sweet:

Yet no wind comes with wings to beat
The silence into sound—but slow
A waving luminous mass doth glow
And palpitate, and stretch, and rise,
And hang suspended in the skies
Until a mighty arch gleams there,
A moonshine-coloured rainbow fair:
Of palest amber is its hue
And delicate as starlit dew,
Till as a silver stream at dawn
Slow stealing through a twilit lawn
It seems to bend and circling flow
Right through the mountain mists below,
And curve again and upward sweep
Till with a flash, a gleam, a leap
The arch becomes a mighty ring
And 'midst the windless mists doth swing.

V. IN THE ANTARCTIC: AT DAYBREAK, BEFORE A STORM.

Hither and thither the icebergs go
With the urgent wind or the current's flow,
And the stormy daydawn pales the fires
That the stars had lit in the frozen spires,
And the amber glow of the midnight moon
Wanes swift in a dim wan silver swoon
From the heart of each iceberg drifting slow
With the wind and the current to and fro,
While the darkling dawn of the colourless day
Breaks o'er a thousand leagues of grey.

And the sunrise coming brings no glad light,
No golden glory, no radiance bright;
But a strait of crimson that gleams blood-red

And an ominous purple overhead
Foretell of the wailing winds that will rise
And sweep on their wild wings through the skies
And howl and shout in their furious chase
Of the waves and clouds in their twin swift race:
And up from the south great masses come drifting,
Night-black and snow-white, falling and lifting,
With quivering rain-lights gleaming and shifting.

But ere the wind and the rain and the hail
Sweep down on the billows whereover we sail,—
Like ghosts from the grave, like spirits that shine
In the garb of their new-born life divine,
From the womb of the clouds, round the brow of the gale
Swift streamers of dazzling light combine,
And flash and shimmer and swing on high
Till five bright rainbows spanning the sky
Of furious tempest prophesy.

And the pinnacled icebergs rock and sway
'Midst rising billows and clouds of spray,
And each holds deep in its frozen mass
A prison'd rainbow—one green as grass,
One blue as a sapphire fill'd with light,
One shining all over with diamonds bright,
One deeply flushing from base to spire
With a glorious ruby's changeful fire,
One all ablaze with an orange gleam—
Till each iceberg there and each wave as well
Are changed by a glorious miracle
To a splendour greater than any dream.

THE WANDERING VOICE.

THEY hear it in the sunless dale,
  It moans beside the stream,
They hear it when the woodlands wail,
  And when the storm-winds scream.

They hear it,—going from the fields
  Through twilight shadows home,—
It sighs across the silent wealds
  And far and wide doth roam.

It moans upon the wind *No more*
  The House of Tredgar stands:
It comes at dusk, and o'er and o'er
  Haunts Tredgar's lands.

He rides down by the foaming linn—
  But hark! what is it calls
With faint far voice, so shrill and thin,
  The House of Tredgar falls.

He lifts the revel-cup at night—
  What makes him start and stare,
What makes his face blanch deadly white,
  What makes him spring from where

His comrades feast within the room,
  And through the darkness go—
What is that wailing cry of doom,
  That scream of woe!

No more in sunless dells, or high
  On moorland ways is heard the moan
Of the long-wandering prophecy:—
  In moonlit nights alone

A shadowy shape is seen to stand
  Beside a ruin'd place:
It waves a wildly threatening hand,
  It hath a dreadful face.

TRANSCRIPTS FROM NATURE. (*Second Series.*)

SECOND SERIES.

I. THE ROOKERY AT SUNRISE.[17]

THE loftly elm-trees darkly dream
   Against the steel-blue sky; till far
   I' the twilit east a golden star
O'erbrims the dusk in one vast stream
Of yellow light, and lo! a cry
Breaks from a windy nest—the sky

Is filled with wheeling rooks—they sway
In one black phalanx towards the day.

II. ON A THAMES BACKWATER.

Its sweeping boughs the great ash trails
    Across the slow-flowing wave: around
    White waterlilies swim; no sound
Disturbs the silence save when sails
On the outer flood a passing boat—
A water-hen quite close doth float,

And, near, a kingfisher's bright gleam
Is mirror'd deep within the stream.

III. OCTOBER WOODLANDS.

Here from this lichen'd crag I see
    The woodlands reach to yonder blues
    Which are the upland downs, in hues
Of gold and red; pale greenery
Yet unstain'd by the sun, and boughs
Of dark-green firs where cushats drowse:

Afar, poised motionless, a pair
Of falcons hover in the air.

IV. THE PINK ACACIA.

Soft clusters mid the shadowy green—
    The pale sea-green acacias make
    When ruffling winds their leaflets shake—
Lie thick and close, as blooms are seen
Upon the pear-tree's boughs in May
Or apple with its blossom-spray:

A flash that melts to pink—such are
Dawn's hues when pales the morning-star.

V. MOUNTAIN-HAZE.

The mountain-haze hides gulf and steep,
    A silver shifting gauzy veil:
    But as the hillside shadows fail
And the glens waken from their sleep,
Soft pink suffuses it—until
It glows all saffron—seems to thrill

    In lucent gold—and then 'tis gone
    And lost where late the sunrise shone.

VI. THE YELLOW POPPY.§§

Like flakes of beaten gold along
    The shingly beach the poppies blow:
    Their sunder'd blossoms to and fro
Are drifted by the wind among
The salt sea-grass, and o'er the wave
That fain this upper beach would lave:

Spring laughs not only o'er the land,
But with her smiles transforms the strand.

VII. MAGNOLIAS. (*Australia.*)

The lofty blue-gums tower on high,
    A giant circle round us here—
    And tree-ferns fringe the little mere
Around whose edge white masses lie,
A thousand snowy blooms o'erbent
With golden hearts and wondrous scent;

---

§§ The beautiful Yellow Horned Poppy is familiar to those who know our southern shores. It is one of the very few flowers, like the Sea-side Convolvulus, the Sand-wort, etc., that grow close to the margin of the sea.

And in the little dark-blue pond
Another bloom-world gleams beyond.

VIII. THE CORAL ISLE.

A calm and waveless purple sea
   Scarce breathes with long slow heavy breath:
   A cloudless sky: 'twould be like death
If rose not yonder faerily
A magic isle with cool green palms,
Adream 'mid coral-girdled calms,

Around whose barriers night and day
The sea-swell breaks in clouds of spray.

IX. GREEN SEAS. (*Terra Del Fuego.*)

With thunder on this iron shore
   The fierce green South Pacific seas
   Break without ceasing: when no breeze
Blows from the icy south they roar
Like famish'd lions, shaking wild
Their foamy manes where rocks are piled:

When tempests ravage, then they grow
Gaunt heralds of resistless woe.

X. FROZEN RAINBOWS. (*Antarctic Icebergs.*)

A north wind fills the straining sails,
   The blue-green sea is creased with white,
   An albatross screams in its flight
And foam-jets rise from spouting whales:
Beyond, around, great icebergs pass,
Some amber, blue, some green as grass,

Some filled with glorious lights—these seem
Like rainbows in a frozen dream.

XI. SUMMER ICEBERGS. (*By Moonlight.*)

The black waves hurry on in hosts,
    Relentless squadrons 'neath the pale
    Cold moon; and thro' the moonshine sail
Great grey wan shapes like island-ghosts:
O'ertoppling, for the seas have laid
Fierce hands upon their bases, made

A hollow sound of waters where
Of late was dead dumb polar air.

XII. THE EVENING STAR. (*At Sea.*)[18]

Aflame with silver fires that glow
    With ruby-change and amethyst,
    Pants, pulses thro' this sundown mist
The even-star, and to and fro
O'er the sea-depths and weedy caves
It dances in a myriad waves,

Though still it thrills and throbs on high,
The sole flame in the purpling sky.

XIII. THE RUINED HILL-TOWER.

A grey old tower of rough-hewn stone,
    Part ivy-clad, with sunlit base
    Where shadow'd branches interlace:
Without, a blue pine stands alone
Above where two stained columns lie,
Memorial of days gone by.

In the mere-waters dark and still
The shadow sleeps of the tower'd hill.

XIV. AN AUTUMNAL EVENING.

Deep black against the dying glow
　　The tall elms stand; the rooks are still;
　　No windbreath makes the faintest thrill
Amongst the leaves; the fields below
Are vague and dim in twilight shades—
Only the bats wheel in their raids

On the grey flies, and silently
Great dusky moths go flitting by.

XV. TRAVELLERS' JOY. (*Trailing Clematis.*)

The trees are leafless now, save where
　　Some shelter'd oak prolongs its dream
　　Of unfled Summer; by the stream
The wither'd sedges show the lair
Of some dead coot; but near the ways
The scarlet hips shine thro' a maze

Of clouded feathery blossoms light,
Which in the sunshine gleam snow-white.

XVI. A CRYSTAL FOREST.[19]

The air is blue and keen and cold,
　　With snow the roads and fields are white;
　　But here the forest's clothed with light
And in a shining sheath enrolled.
Each branch, each twig, each blade of grass,
Seems clad miraculously with glass:

Above the ice-bound streamlet bends
Each frozen fern with crystal ends.

XVII. THE MOORS. (*September.*)

A sky of rich deep blue: beneath,
   A mighty sterile mountain-range;
   Far west with shifting shades doth change
The sea; all else is purple heath—
A glorious purple world wherein
A myriad lives each morn begin,

Where the grouse call, and the grey hare
Leaps, and whirling curlews fill the air.

XVIII. THE DEAD STAG.

Upon the purple moor quite dead
   The antlered monarch lonely lies,
   The proud fire vanisht from his eyes;
The mountain-sunset burns blood-red,
And makes the tarn beside the stag
Flame like an outstretched crimson flag:

Two hooded crows their wings flap near,
Not long to be kept back by fear.

XIX. THE HAUNT OF THE OSPREY.

(*Western Highlands.*)

A rugged scaur in the mid-lake
   Stands high and peak'd; on this doth rest
   The ragged semblance of a nest;
Here the young birds their hunger slake

With fish the parent ospreys bring,
Here they shriek loud their hungering;

Here the sea-eagles breed, and here
As savage chiefs they rule through fear.

XX. THE BLASTED PINE.

The barren granite cliffs withstand
    The Atlantic surge that day and night
    Breaks in the thunder of its might:
And on the furthest spur of land—
A mighty fissured crag—rears high
A blasted pine against the sky:

Dead, lightning-riven, black, alone,
Its bare boughs answer the wind's moan.

XXI. SUMMER YELLOWS.

The hill-side shimmers with live gold
    Of scented gorse; the celandine
    Lights up the lanes; o'er meadows green
Kingcups and daffodils have rolled
A sunshine wave; and by the stream
Marsh-mallows and tall iris gleam:

With sweet wild song the goldfinch flies,
And oft the yellowhammer cries.

XXII. AN AFTERGLOW AMID THE CUMBERLAND FELLS.
(*December*, 1883.)

Gloom shrouds the hills and hides the dales,
    The wintry sun an hour has set:
    But lo! a blood-red parapet

Leans from the sky, and crimson veils
Of stealthy vapour cling and crawl
About the night's funereal pall—

Till with a wind it seems to sway
And drift in burning flakes away.

XXIII. A WINTER HEDGEROW.

The wintry wolds are white; the wind
    Seems frozen; in the shelter'd nooks
    The sparrows shiver; the black rooks
Wheel homeward where the elms behind
The manor stand; at the field's edge
The redbreasts in the blackthorn hedge

Sit close, and under snowy eaves
The shrewmice sleep 'mid nested leaves.

XXIV. WILD SWANS. (*Western Isles.*)

An inland strait of the salt sea
    Lost in a purple wilderness
    Where seldom wandering feet transgress:
Low rainy hills stand mournfully
Amid the wide drear waste—and where
The sea-loch laps their bases bare

The wild-swans with the dying light
Wheel, screaming, in their phalanx'd flight.

XXV. THE SALMON POOL.

The tassell'd birch o'erhangs the pool,
    Clear amber, where the pebbles shine
    Like opals amid golden wine;

And where the margin dark and cool
Reflects a tremulous world of green
The thrush from its lithe spray has seen

A band of living silver lie
Deep down in moveless symmetry.

XXVI. THE EAGLE. (*Western Highlands.*)

Between two mighty hills a sheer
    Abyss—far down in the ravine
    A thread-like torrent and a screen
Of oaks like shrubs—and one doth rear
A dry scarp'd peak above all sound
Save windy voices wailing round:

At sunrise here, in proud disdain,
The eagle scans his vast domain.

MADONNA NATURA.

I love and worship thee in that thy ways
Are fair, and that the glory of past days
    Haloes thy brightness with a sacred hue:
Within thine eyes are dreams of mystic things,
Within thy voice a subtler music rings
    Than ever mortal from the keen reeds drew;
Thou weav'st a web which men have called Death
But Life is in the magic of thy breath.

The secret things of Earth thou knowest well;
Thou seest the wild-bee build his narrow cell,
    The lonely eagle wing through lonely skies,
The lion on the desert roam afar,
The glow-worm glitter like a fallen star,

The hour-lived insect as it hums and flies;
Thou seest men like shadows come and go,
And all their endless dreams drift to and fro.

In thee is strength, endurance, wisdom, truth:
Thou art above all mortal joy and ruth,
    Thou hast the calm and silence of the night:
Mayhap thou seest what we cannot see,
Surely far off thou hear'st harmoniously
    Echoes of flawless music infinite,
Mayhap thou feelest thrilling through each sod
Beneath thy feet the very breath of God.

Monna Natura, *fair and grand and great,*
I worship thee, who art inviolate:
    Through thee I reach to things beyond the span
Of mine own puny life, through thee I learn
Courage and hope, and dimly can discern
    The ever nobler grades awaiting man:
Madonna, unto thee I bend and pray—
Saviour, Redeemer thou, whom none can slay!

No human fanes are dedicate to thee,
But thine the temples of each tameless sea,
    Each mountain-height and forest-glade and plain:
No priests with daily hymns thy praises sing,
But far and wide the wild winds chanting swing,
    And dirge the sea-waves on the changeless main,
While songs of birds fill all the fields and woods,
And cries of beasts the savage solitudes.

Hearken, Madonna, hearken to my cry:
Teach me through metaphors of liberty,
    Till strong and fearing nought in life or death
I feel thy sacred freedom through me thrill,
Wise, and defiant, with unquenched will

Unyielding, though succumb the mortal breath—
Then if I conquer take me by the hand
And guide me onward to thy Promised Land!

NOTES.

1. Transcript No. IV., p. 58. As Mr. W. Stokes has pointed out (*Academy*, 16th February, 1884), Tennyson, when referring to the kingfisher as 'the sea-blue bird of March,' in Stanza xci. of *In Memoriam*, has evidently taken the phrase from Alcman, who, in his twelfth fragment, uses an identical Greek phrase. Voss, in his hexametrical translation, speaks of it as the *purpurner vogel des frühlings*.

See also subsequent suggestions in the *Academy* (15th March) in favour of the wheatear, the blue titmouse, and the swallow: but there is little doubt that both Alcman and the Laureate meant the kingfisher.

2. Transcripts Nos. V. and VI., and p. 122—While the fireflies of Italy are invariably of flame colour, varying from red to pale crimson, and even to faint orange, those I have seen in more northern latitudes—as in the Ardennes and the Province of Luxembourg—have as invariably been green, as well as generally less resplendent. The farther south, the warmer the clime, the more brilliant are these 'wandering fires.'

3. *Gaspara Stampa*, Pt. I. San Salvatore is where the Lords of Collalto had their seignorial residence. The name 'Cadore' in the ninth line is Anglicised from *Cadōré*.

4. *Gaspara Stampa*, Pt. II., lines 15 to 30. *Irene* here refers to the beautiful Irene of Spilemburg: *Violante Palma* was that lovely daughter of the famous painter of the same surname, whose portraiture the latter has transmitted to us in many paintings, but most memorably in the beautiful 'Sta. Barbara' in the Church of Sta. Maria della Formosa, in Venice: *Cornelia* was Titian's sister: *Molino* was a well-known poet in his time, and of course the names of Sansovino, Varchi, Cardinal Bembo, and Pietro Aretino require no comment.

5. *Gaspara Stampa*, Pt. II. The foregoing lines are based on the fine painting by Mr. Eugene Benson, entitled *An August Evening at Titian's Home, Venice*, exhibited at the Royal Academy in 1882.

6. *Gaspara Stampa*, Pt. II. Song on page 75, beginning *I gaze into thine eyes*, is founded on the fifth and fourth of the Sonnets by Gaspara as translated

by 'George Fleming.' I have kept as literally as practicable to the latter's more measured rendering.

7. *Gaspara Stampa*, Pt. III., line 22. The meaning of the opening lines of Gaspara's ninth Sonnet.

8. *Gaspara Stampa*, Pt. IV. Song on page 82 is almost literally the beautiful rendering by 'George Fleming' of Sonnet VI. Here the two closing lines have no prototypes in that sonnet, but such are to be found elsewhere amongst Gaspara's sonnets or madrigals.

9. *Sonnets on Paintings by Bazzi* (*Sodona*). I have elsewhere (*Art Journal*, April, 1884) pointed out the advisability of either invariably calling this great artist by his right name, or else using what was probably the name he assumed when (like Titian) he was made a Count Palatine—viz., *Sodona*. Vasari's nickname should now be forgotten, if on no other account than on the principle of *De mortuis*, etc.

10. Page 90. The Water-Joy (from the generic name of the flower, which is from the Greek words 'water' and 'to rejoice') is the Lesser Water Lily, or, as it is commonly called, 'Frog-Bit.' The latter name is in reference to the haunts of this plant: in Germany also it is called *Der Froschbiss*. Its thick masses of white stars render pools and streams doubly beautiful, and none more so than the lovely Lesse, which flows into the Meuse at Anseremme, near Dinant.

11. Page 102. The Shea-Oak (Casuarina) has long drooping filaments instead of leaves. The sound these give forth on a stormy day is extremely mournful, heightened by the dreariness of the surrounding tracts.

11*a*. Page 102 Transcript No. V. The giant lizard (here referred to), the 'Monitor,' or *Hydrasaurus varius*, varies from four to six feet in length. Although it can bite severely, it is not harmful to man. When there is not a sound from any living thing to be heard in the forest, when even the bell-birds are silenced, and the scorpions and centipedes are torpid in the furnace-heat, the monitor basks upon some spreading bough, motionless for hours, but ready in a moment for any restless beetle or other insect that may come his way. The first time I saw one (116° in the shade) it literally seemed to *radiate* heat, but it was probably impervious to the fiery breath of noon to which it lay fully exposed.

12. Page 103. Only those who have witnessed the beautiful phenomenon referred to in the final couplet can have any true idea of its exquisite loveliness.

156

This mysterious veil of translucent blue clothes the Austral hill-ranges only for a few wonderful moments during the brief twilight that is just long enough to form a recognisable interlude between day and night.

13. Page 103. The 'Flying Mouse' here referred to is not a bat, but one of the *Phalangistæ*. The Phalangers of Australia are different from the opossums of America. The Flying Mouse is the smallest of the so-called flying opossums—and indeed is one of the smallest animals in creation—Wallace mentioning that 'it could go to sleep in a good-sized pill-box.'

14. Page 104. The Rock-lily (*Doryanthes excelsa*) has a flower-stalk thirty feet high, crowned with lily-like blooms of a rich dark-red hue, and several feet in circumference.

15. Page 104. The *Brachychiton acerifolium*, or 'flame-tree' of the colonists, when covered with its large crimson blooms, is a most beautiful sight, especially when seen *en masse*. In the right season, the Illawarra mountain range (on the eastern side of New South Wales) is said to be conspicuous for miles at sea by reason of the glowing crimson of these flame-trees in full flower.

16. Page 138. The scientific name given to this remarkable phenomenon.

17. Transcript No. I., p. 143. A remarkable occurrence which, circumstances being favourable, any one may see for himself who would think the sight worth rising for before day-dawn. Shelley had seen it at least once, as is evident by his graphic passage in the *Lines written amongst the Euganean Hills*. Mr. Stopford Brooke, also, in the notes to his delightful volume of Selections from Shelley, records having himself witnessed the spectacle.

18. Page 147. Since this Transcript was written I find that in a poem called 'Even Star,' in his pleasant volume *Io in Egypt: and other Poems*, Mr. Richard Garnett has expressed the same *motif* much more successfully. The lines to which I refer are these:

> "The grey sky sparkles with my fairy light;
> I mix among the dancers of the sea,
> Yet stoop not from the throne I must retain
> High o'er the silver sources of the rain.'

19. Page 148, Transcript No. XVI. In Canada, Norway, Scotland, and other northern countries, this beautiful winter-transformation can frequently

be seen. It is caused by intense frost setting in immediately upon a thaw, thus congealing the damp upon even the tiniest twigs and blades of grass and fern-fronds into sheaths of thin transparent crystal. As the sun's heat intensifies, the crackling and dripping are incessant, and the change and beauty beyond description.

Printed by BoD™in Norderstedt, Germany

9 781396 320187